THE LEARN-IT-ALL LEADER

THE LEARN·IT·ALL LEADER

LEADER

mindset, traits & tools

Damon Lembi

LIONCREST

PUBLISHING

THE LEARN-IT-ALL LEADER

Mindset, Traits & Tools

FIRST EDITION

ISBN   978-1-5445-4165-5   *Hardcover*

        978-1-5445-4163-1   *Paperback*

        978-1-5445-4164-8   *Ebook*

To Lucy and Wally,

This book is for you. I want to make both of you proud of your parents like I am of mine; I love you two so much.

CONTENTS

INTRODUCTION

On a typical ninety-degree desert night in the spring of 1995, I was up next to bat for Arizona State. It was the Saturday of alumni weekend, so the stands were a little fuller and a bit less focused on the game, but I was all in. This was my second year with the team and our first season in twenty-three years playing without our legendary coach, Jim Brock, and I knew his widow Pat was in the stands. We'd been playing well but at the bottom of the fourth, we were down two runs with runners on first and third, and I was looking for my turn to drive in a run or two.

As I took a couple of practice swings, I heard a voice behind me. "Hey, Lembi! Hey, number twenty!"

I turned around. There, in the front row, behind the on-deck circle, was Barry Bonds, Arizona State's most famous alumnus and third on ESPN's "Baseball's Hall of 100" after only Babe Ruth and Willie Mays. He waved me over (*Me? Is he waving at me?*) with a gruff, "Listen up."

I was listening. I was thrilled and surprised and, to be honest, possibly in shock, but I was listening. I don't think I even said, "Yeah?" or "What?" to the man, just nodded.

"Look at the pitcher," Bonds said. "When he squeezes his glove, he's throwing a fastball. When he holds his glove flat, it's a curveball. Got it?"

I got it and walked to the plate muttering, "Squeeze, fastball. Flat, curveball."

The pitcher squeezed his glove, I prepared for a fastball, swung, and missed. On the next pitch, I got it wrong again. "Screw it," I thought. "Barry can see things I can't (that's why he's Barry). I'm going back to my normal approach." On the next pitch, I hit a double into the gap.

From second base, I looked into the stands and got two thumbs up from Mr. Barry Bonds. I was thrilled. Years later, I'd get to know him. My brother, dad, and I were even traveling with him when he broke Hank Aaron's historic home run record, and his tip and my complete failure to capitalize on it became a running joke with us. But he taught me much more that day than the tells of a particular pitcher.

Barry Bonds, at a college ball game, was studying a pitcher he'd never face. He was watching intently, developing theories, and testing them out. On a day off and out of town, he was still—always—a student of the game. Barry Bonds pulled all the information he could glean from every game he watched or played to make himself a better player.

But learning wasn't all he did. Without any skin in that game, he still took the trouble to flag me down, call me over, and offer me some coaching. He'd learned something, and he wanted me to learn it too.

Years later, after my baseball career ended, the experience came back to me as an example of what it means to be both a student and a leader. I don't think I could have put it into words at the time, but I internalized it. Several years into a twenty-two-year-long career, Barry was watching that college ball game with committed curiosity, extracting lessons from it, and sharing those lessons with me.

That's what it means to be a learn-it-all leader.

You may be familiar with the opposite; know-it-alls aren't in short supply. Whether through defensiveness, confidence, or disinterest, know-it-alls are set in their ways, have a fixed mindset, and are averse to change. I've met know-it-all baseball coaches and seasoned senior executives who thought they knew everything there was to know about baseball or business. And many of them did, in fact, know a lot—more than I did. I, however, know more now than I used to, and they've plateaued. Know-it-alls can achieve a degree of success (although plenty don't), but the most respected and resilient leaders I've known, no matter their length of tenure or academic pedigree, have been learn-it-alls. It's the one trait that seems to guarantee progress. Today, it may just be table stakes.

The way we work is rapidly changing. The onset of the COVID-19 pandemic brought about a significant increase in remote and hybrid work, and even before 2019, advances in artificial intelligence (AI) were driving the automation of more and more of our task-driven work. This isn't bad news! All three previous Industrial Revolutions eventually created more jobs than they eliminated. But the nature of those jobs substantively changed each time, and the same is likely to be true for us. As automation and AI take over much of our repetitive, tedious, and routine work, we'll be both freer and more required to do the kind of work that machines don't do well—work that calls on our uniquely human capacities to innovate, adapt, make nuanced judgments, think critically, and learn.

I saw this incipient global trend play out recently on the microscale in the accounting department of Learnit. Learnit is a training company that helps organizations develop the hard and soft skills their people want now and will need in the future through online and in-person educational classes. As its CEO, I was leading an initiative to automate our accounts-receivable processes, when Michelle, a member of our in-house accounting team, pulled me aside. "If Learnit is automating over 50 percent of my workload, is there still a role for me here?"

Michelle is a forward-thinker and an incredible team player. She's smart, savvy, and an excellent communicator—the kind of person we want to keep and develop. I told her that even though her role was changing, she was still valuable to our team and we would work hard to pivot her current role to focus on her strengths in a way that would benefit both her and the company.

"But with all the new automation handling most of my existing tasks," she asked, "will what I do still be relevant?"

I answered her question with a question (a learn-it-all move). "Michelle, given your experience and knowledge of Learnit, how do you think we can better leverage your strengths to improve the company? Are there any areas of focus you'd like to upskill in?"

She didn't even have to think about it. "I'd love to learn data modeling," she told me. "I think it'd be cool to learn Power BI and maybe even attend our *Storytelling with Data* workshops. I could see myself presenting one day at our quarterly all-hands meetings, and who knows, maybe even at a board meeting one day!"

"Great," I said. "Let's make it happen! I'd love for you to help our executive team better understand the numbers and get us to the point where we can forecast revenue trends by product line and profitability by customer."

One of Learnit's core values is lifelong learning. We've created a culture of people with a strong desire to reskill and upskill and have the resources in place to allow them to do so. It's one of the lures we use to recruit A-level players like Michelle. It's also one of the tests we use to screen out the B-level players who look more like learn-it-alls on paper than they are in real life. (There's more on how Learnit hires for learn-it-alls in Chapter 6.)

I'd like to tell you I walked in on day one at Learnit able to articulate the mindset, practices, and principles of learn-it-all leadership (I'd also like to tell you I can still hit a 100-mph pitch and fit into my college uniform), but I became a learn-it-all leader because I worked there. Twenty-plus years of leading a learning company contributed to, shaped, and helped codify how I think, what I do, and how I keep learning. The company's name became my personal mission.

I believe anyone who wants to excel in today's business climate (much less in the automated and AI-assisted future) needs to be a learn-it-all. If Michelle hadn't advocated for a new role, she would have become irrelevant and eventually lost her job. It takes the kind of growth mindset and innovative thinking she displayed to level up and get what you want in any career, but it's particularly critical for leaders. Leaders who think they know it all can't compete in the marketplace, attract great talent, or keep the people they hire.

Because learning drives innovation and adaptation, know-it-all leaders are quickly outpaced by their more learning-oriented competitors. Leaders who weren't curious in early 2020 about how a global pandemic might impact their business are out of business. The Great Resignation of 2021 was driven, at least in part, by employees who were fed up with their leaders' inability to adapt appropriately. It's the contemporary equivalent of Blockbuster turning down the opportunity to buy Netflix for $50 million in 2000 because the Blockbuster CEO could only see Netflix as "a very small niche business."[1] By the end of 2022, it was worth over $300 million.[2] Excusing a refusal to change with "that's the way we've always done things" is like trying to run mergers and acquisitions like a cattle raid. And just as deadly. A lack of curiosity at the highest levels of an organization not only blinds the company to new dangers, it casts a shadow over the entire organization. Leaders, deliberately or not, lead by example.

Learn-it-all leaders indirectly model and directly encourage a culture of learning inside their organizations. This attracts higher-quality workers, improves their performance over time, and holds onto them longer.

Workers have probably always wanted to learn and grow on the job. Even Ford's famously rigid assembly lines probably had the occasional employee who tried something new. But millennials are as famous for their desire to get much more than a paycheck from their jobs. Today's twenty-somethings and new entries into the job market expect to have opportunities to continue learning and growing, and they leave jobs that fail to meet that expectation.

In short, know-it-all leaders find themselves with no business to run

---

1   Marc Graser, "Epic Fail: How Blockbuster Could Have Owned Netflix," *Variety*, November 12, 2013, https://variety.com/2013/biz/news/epic-fail-how-blockbuster-could-have-owned-netflix-1200823443/.

2   "Netflix Current Valuation," Macroaxis, accessed January 5, 2023, https://www.macroaxis.com/invest/ratio/NFLX/Current-Valuation.

and no one to run it, while learn-it-all leaders see change coming and adapt quickly. Because they model and support learning across their organizations, they attract and lead steadily more knowledgeable and skillful workers. Not only are employees of such companies happier and more engaged, they're a rich resource for their leaders, allowing them to promote from within, thus preserving institutional wisdom.

This isn't a new idea. Learn-it-alls have long been at the head of great companies and at the front lines of history's most pivotal moments. Winston Churchill and Joe Montana are my favorite examples. While they may not seem to have much in common, they were both extraordinary learners. As profootballhistory.com has pointed out, Joe Montana didn't look like anything special. He was skinny, didn't have a cannon for an arm, wasn't particularly fast, and had only average mechanics.

It took Winston Churchill three tries to get into a military college (which he hated), and his disastrous failures in Turkey and Norway suggest the schools might have had good reason for rejecting him. Neither man was exceptionally gifted or naturally adept in the fields they eventually dominated. Their victories were learned.

And you don't have to take my word for it. Here's what Joe Montana had to say about learning. "We're all going to make mistakes, so the biggest thing is how you recover from that mistake. What do you do? Do you put so much pressure on yourself that you compound it and make it worse? Take a step back and consider, 'What did I do? What caused that?'"[3]

The imminently quotable Churchill gives us almost too many rele-

---

3   Rachel Lee, "Lifelong Learning Insights with Joe Montana," *WorkRamp* (blog), September 9, 2022, https://www.workramp.com/blog/lifelong-learning-insights-with-joe-montana/.

vant options to choose from. Most famously, "Those that fail to learn from history are doomed to repeat it." Or, almost as famously and with a bit of bonus wry wit, "I'm always ready to learn, although I do not always like being taught." Finally, and to my next point, "My education was interrupted only by my schooling."

When I was in high school, if you'd told me I'd one day be CEO of a learning and development organization, I don't think I would have believed you. Major League Baseball player? Sure. Husband and father? Absolutely. I would probably have even believed I might eventually become the Guns N' Roses road manager (more on that later). But being immersed in the learning and development world for twenty-seven-plus years? I probably would have just laughed. As a teen, I hadn't yet figured out the difference between school and education. I expected to graduate high school and go to college, but I wasn't what anyone would call a scholar. I was spending most of my attention and passion on baseball.

Do I wish I'd distributed my hours a little differently? Sure. Did I get an excellent education? Absolutely. I learned at least half of what I needed to know from coaches and most of the rest from my parents and other mentors throughout my life. Very little of my real education was learned in classrooms from professors. I was an avid student, but not much of a scholar. The critical difference isn't where you learn—on the field or in the classroom. It's one of mindset and habit, ideas and actions.

Scholars have a less aggressive relationship with information. They're receivers and retainers. They acquire knowledge and hold onto it. They learn—thoroughly and reliably—what they're taught, whether they're particularly interested in it or not. They do well on tests. They make great managers.

Great leaders are great students, and the world is their classroom. They're information extractors. They pull what they learn about everything—be it product innovation or how to inspire a team—from their lived experience. Some of those experiences may happen in a classroom but many don't. This kind of learner pulls lessons from everywhere, everyone, and everything.

As an example, if work were a family vacation, the leader is the one who dreams up the trip—where you'll go, the sites you'll see, cool side quests for the kids—and talks up the trip until at least one of you is too excited to sleep. A leader creates the itinerary and sets the dates. The manager makes sure the flights and hotels are booked.

Some people are both students and scholars, able to extract information from experience and hold onto everything they've been explicitly taught (tricks for this in Chapter 9). Typically, however, people are either extractors or collectors by temperament—and our schools are set up only for the latter. Since this is a book about learning and not the American school system (which is different from an education system), I'll just point out that it teaches, tests on, and rewards the collection, retention, and regurgitation of information that's been explicitly taught. Much of which is freely available on the internet. I'll also mention, in passing, that anything that can be taught and tested this way can also be "learned" by AI, making this kind of learning less valuable.

A more immediate effect of this mismatch between extractors and schools is the large number of mediocre students who could become great leaders and don't. If they do, it happens much more slowly and with a lot more imposter syndrome and negative self-talk than their equally intelligent but more scholarly peers. If you recognize yourself in that description, I wrote this book for you. I want you to know, right here in the Introduction, before the book even begins, that you can be a great learn-it-all leader even if you weren't rewarded as a scholar.

Some learn-it-alls fall into leadership roles because their restless information-seeking and hands-on experimentation led to the formation of their own company which needed somebody to run it. The rest come up through the ranks, where it can be harder to tell the difference between leaders and managers. They're usually either the encumbered extractors we've already talked about or natural scholars who—whether they know it or not—have just been promoted out of their element. If you're one of this breed and want to become a learn-it-all, I wrote this book for you too. This book is also for you if you're an experienced leader looking to up your learn-it-all game or a learn-it-all who is (of course) in the habit of reading new business books because, well, that's who you are.

I've broken learn-it-all leadership into two aspects: being and doing (or ideas and actions). Part 1 of *The Learn-It-All Leader* explores how we think. I lay out the four components of a learn-it-all mindset—commitment, humility, curiosity, and humanity—and offer some suggestions for how to further develop and strengthen those traits. In Part 2, I examine what learn-it-alls do differently—they take bolder risks, make better decisions, build stronger teams, play to win, and coach their players.

Great leaders aren't born. They're not made either. They're *in the making*. They're constantly creating and re-creating themselves, their companies, and their leadership. It isn't something that can be done from the sidelines. You need to be committed.

PART 1

BEING

CHAPTER 1

GO ALL IN

One of my earliest memories is of the time I insisted that my preschool teacher call me Batman. Like most kids, I loved superheroes and had a lively imagination. Batman was my favorite. He was who I wanted to be. He was who I was. Why wasn't everyone already calling me Batman?

We still have the letter my preschool teacher sent my parents: "Dear Mr. and Mrs. Lembi, your son is a lively and polite young man, but he will only respond if we call him Batman."

My parents didn't see the problem. They saw that I was fully committed to being Batman with all my preschool intensity and muscle power, and they were okay with that. They were somewhat less understanding when I committed with equal fervor to protesting the arrival of my baby sister. I'd wanted a brother, and when one failed to materialize, I painted the imposter red to call attention to the error.

I'm not here to recommend we all insist on being addressed by our superhero names and I've since learned the tremendous value of having a sister. (My sister Sammy has been one of my top confidants through the years and a wonderful, caring "Auntie Sammy" to our children. I love her dearly.) I've also come to value the intensity of my childhood passionate commitment. This is in part, I believe, because I lost touch with it for a few years and had to relearn it.

BE COMMITTED

Learn-it-all leaders go all in. They work with passion and intensity. They create a compelling vision and commit fully to it. But they don't necessarily do this naturally. There are things that get in the way of going all in. More accurately, there are ways of getting in your own way that drain you of your passion and commitment. The two that tripped me up the most after I outgrew my bat cape were the particular breed of low self-confidence that's often called "imposter syndrome" and another syndrome I call "the lucky curse." I learned to deal with them both at Arizona State. Later, I learned that they're both subsets of something that's even harder to fight—fear.

IMPOSTER SYNDROME

In high school, I played both baseball and basketball, but at six foot two and without much of a vertical leap, I decided baseball was my best chance of going pro. I went all in, working extremely hard. It paid off. I made all-state, got to travel to South Korea and play alongside several major league players, and was recruited by top college baseball programs including the University of Southern California (USC), Oklahoma State, and Pepperdine. 1990 was an exciting time for me.

But it was also decision time—and I had a big one to make. I'd been offered a baseball scholarship and a starting position playing third base at Pepperdine University. I was attracted to the school by the vision its coach, Andy Lopez, had for the team and for how I could contribute to his plans for winning the college world series. But I'd also been drafted by the Atlanta Braves in the thirteenth round of the MLB draft. The pressure was intense to figure out which path—minor league baseball or the opportunity to play for one of the premier college programs in the country—was best for me.

My parents generously gave me full autonomy to make whichever decision I thought best. Maybe the choice seems obvious to you, but at the time—I just froze. At seventeen, was I ready for minor-league life? Would going to college improve my position in the draft in future years? If I didn't go pro now, could I be sure I'd get another chance? I couldn't decide. I went back and forth, torturing myself for a while before finally deciding on Pepperdine.

I'd like to be able to say that my decision was based on wanting to get an education, but the truth is that I was just a seventeen-year-old kid, and I was scared. I made a decision, but I didn't fully commit. I wasn't sure that I was ready for either option. Imposter syndrome[4] had me questioning my own abilities.

As a little kid, when I'd wanted to be Batman, I'd just owned it. I claimed it with confidence even though I knew I wasn't really that powerful. Stepping onto the college field with some of the top college baseball players in the country, I wasn't sure I belonged. I

---

4   Imposter syndrome is a crippling lack of self-confidence that can profoundly affect performance or, in the words of Wikipedia, "a psychological occurrence in which an individual doubts their skills, talents, or accomplishments and has a persistent internalized fear of being exposed as a fraud."

doubted my ability and didn't claim my right to be there the way I'd owned my (more ambiguous) right to be called Batman.

In the preseason, I struggled to find my stride, which didn't do my confidence any favors. I was questioning my decision. I was home-sick. By midseason, it was obvious to me and everybody else that I wasn't cutting it. Coach Lopez sat me down and didn't mince words. "When we recruited you, Damon, I thought you would be a great third baseman, but to be honest, now I'm not so sure."

As I sat there listening to him, in my mind I started planning the quickest way out—fly or rent a U-Haul? Did I have to take every-thing with me, or could I ship stuff home? But Coach Lopez wasn't done. "Maybe you're not a good fit for Pepperdine," he went on, watching me closely.

I couldn't argue with the man. Maybe there was a flight out that afternoon. I could just leave my stuff.

And Coach Lopez *still* wasn't done. He paused for a second. Then he said, "That's not what I believe, Damon. But it's what's in your head and that is what matters. I believe you have the talent and the ability to be a great third baseman and eventually a high draft choice, but my opinion won't matter if you don't believe it too. It takes talent and hard work *and* confidence to succeed at this level."

I had the talent and work ethic, but I was missing that final piece. Imposter syndrome had me in its clutches. My past success wasn't enough to prove my abilities to me. I didn't feel like I belonged on the team. I felt like an imposter.

I wish I could say I took Coach Lopez's words to heart and immediately turned the season and my career at Pepperdine around. But I didn't. I'd like to believe I would have had bad luck not intervened, but it did. I suffered a season-ending injury. It took me a while to understand what he'd taught me, but Coach Lopez was right. You can't substitute other people's belief in you for belief in yourself. Only you can put the "self" in "self-confidence."

Coach Lopez taught me to spot the imposter syndrome in myself, and I've seen it since in others, including highly successful and valued members of my team. Several years ago Jennifer Albrecht, our VP of Training, and I had the great fortune to attend the Ritz Carlton's *Culture of Excellence* program inside Pentagon City. The Ritz brought in several outside consultants with extensive business coaching and leadership experience. For me, it was one of the best learning experiences I've ever had. For Jen, it was transformational. I watched as, throughout the week, she was asked to lead more and more sessions. It reminded me of seeing Guns N' Roses open up for the Stones at the Coliseum in 1989—her opening act outperformed experienced stars—and I realized how fortunate Learnit was to have her on our team.

On one of the final afternoons, Jen and I took a walk together around the Lincoln Memorial in DC. "You know," she said, "I've always wanted to start teaching leadership classes at Learnit, but as a young woman still early in my career, I didn't feel like I measured up to other companies' leadership instructors with their suits and ties and twenty-plus years of experience. But you know what, Damon? We can f**king do this!"

"One hundred percent we can!" I told her.

And we did.

I'll take some credit for egging her on, but it was the Ritz program that showed Jen she wasn't just as good as the other instructors there—she was better. For her, this company-funded opportunity to learn and grow led to a personal breakthrough that gave her enough confidence to drive herself to meet her full potential. We left that four-day event with new inspiration for our leadership program and with multiple other job opportunities for Jen which, happily for us, she chose to turn down. I am forever grateful for both her and the Ritz. It was a game-changing four days for Learnit. We'd offered leadership classes previously but were seen primarily as a computer training organization. Jen's increased confidence helped expand the company's reputation as a trusted partner for all of our customers' learning and development (L&D) needs.

BEATING IMPOSTER SYNDROME

Even without a Ritz Carlton *Culture of Excellence* program or a Coach Lopez, you can still stop imposter syndrome from tripping you up or standing in your way. It takes three things: hard work, focus, and learning.

1. Hard Work

You don't need to work a fourteen-hour day, seven days a week, but you do have to put in consistent hard work. The old cliché is true; there are no shortcuts on the road to success, but more importantly, putting in the effort builds not just the skills you'll need but also your confidence in those skills. At Arizona State, I was the first one at practice and the last one to leave. Everyday. Knowing I'd done that was what convinced me I'd earned my position and belonged on the team.

2. Focus

It's hard to feel confident about anything when your attention is being pulled in every direction. Whether it's through external interruptions or internal resistance, there are always obstacles in your way as you try to achieve your goals. Maintaining a laser focus on those goals helps build the self-confidence needed to leave impostor syndrome behind. (We'll talk more about the relationship between focus and goals in the next section.)

3. Learning

Keep learning top of mind and constantly look for ways to improve to reinforce your confidence. A passion for learning and the persistence to follow through on gaining the skills that you need to reach your goals will go a long way toward defeating impostor syndrome.

THE LUCKY CURSE

Our parents didn't spoil my siblings and me, but from a young age, I was aware that some people saw our privilege (and we were definitely privileged) as fundamentally unfair. I'll be the first to acknowledge the serious perks of growing up as part of a wealthy and well-known family, but there's also a downside—my wins could always be attributed to advantage and explained away. Even though my parents didn't hire a team of specialist coaches and nutritionists or build out our house with professional training equipment, I knew some people thought I was doing well only because of the opportunities I'd been born into.

Such assumptions about the impact of your family background can eat away at your confidence until you realize that no matter where you come from—privilege or poverty—when you step up to the plate, you're the one who has to perform, not your parents or your past. I think for a while I bought into the idea that I was just lucky. I *was* lucky, but it wasn't just luck that accounted for my success.

Whether it's a supportive family or natural talent, every advantage brings with it the weight of expectation. After my injury, I was worried about letting down the people who believed in me (especially my dad), and I put a lot of pressure on myself. After a lot of doubt and uncertainty, I decided Pepperdine wasn't the right fit for me and went to play junior college ball at the College of San Mateo for John Noce, one of the winningest coaches in junior college baseball history.

As a highly regarded prospect, there were a lot of expectations on me. I felt the pressure of them and was still dealing with my disappointment about how things had worked out at Pepperdine. But I had a solid career at San Mateo and my confidence gradually increased under Coach Noce, who helped get me a chance to play in the Cape Cod Baseball League with some of the greatest players of my generation (Todd Helton, Aaron Boone, and Nomar Garciaparra to name a few). Halfway through the summer league season, I was about to commit to Oklahoma State University when I got a call from Arizona State. Their first baseman (Paul Lo Duca) had signed with the Dodgers and they needed a new one. There was no guarantee I would be the starting first baseman if I signed with them, but the opportunity was there.

Some of my friends thought I was crazy to even think about it. "Damon, it's ASU, one of the top three programs in the country," they reminded me. "They'll have twenty guys trying out for first base. Why not go to a smaller program or a Division 2 school where you have some assurance you'll get to play?" I thought about what they had to say, but I wasn't a scared kid anymore. I'd learned to believe in myself enough to take a risk. I felt like Arizona State was my last shot at a baseball career, so I took the leap. I went all in. I stopped worrying about what other people thought. I quit caring about the risk of failure. I made the decision to do everything I could, put in the work, give it my best shot, and let the cards fall where they may.

By the year I joined the team, Jim Brock, the legendary head coach for ASU, already had two College World Series Championships and four national Coach of the Year awards under his belt. He was also in the final stages of liver cancer heading into what would be his last season, and he was struggling. Some days he wouldn't make it out to the field at all. But when he wasn't feeling too bad from the chemo treatments, he'd come out and sit there in his chair, and his presence would inspire us. He modeled so much courage just by showing up.

We were ranked in the top ten nationally preseason, and I had won the starting first base position. When we lost the first two games of an early season series at Florida State, I expected Coach Brock to really let us have it, but he didn't. He just told us to go back to the hotel.

We were a bunch of frustrated college kids in a great college town, so you can probably imagine what happened next. We hit the bars and stayed out way too late. At five the next morning, none of us were prepared for the pounding fist on the door and the order to grab our shoes and head down to the field.

Coach Brock was there. I don't remember whether we showed up feeling ashamed or scared or just really hungover. I do remember he ran us. Hard. Then he lined us up. I'm sure we were a sorry sight, panting and green. Coach walked down the line and laid into us. He started with our third baseman (who went on to be the fourth overall pick in the 1994 draft). "You came here as one of the top prospects in the country. You're lazy and you don't do shit," Coach told him.

He moved on to our shortstop. "You're working really hard. You're doing great."

To the next guy, "You were better as a freshman than you are now. You're embarrassing yourself out there."

I started wondering what he was going to say when he got to me. After all, at the game the night before I had gone 0-for-4 with two strikeouts and an error.

He said, "Lembi, you're a slow-footed, slow-thinking sloth. If you don't pull your head out of your ass, you're not going to be on the bench, you will be on the next plane back to Burlingame!"

I think it's safe to say we all got the message loud and clear.[5]

That afternoon, I stepped up to the plate in the first inning knowing my grandfather, Frank Lembi, was there in the crowd at Dick Howser Stadium. A shrewd, no-nonsense World War II vet, he'd built our San Francisco real estate empire from scratch but couldn't tell a baseball bat from a hockey stick. Famous for never showing an ounce of fear over anything, he watched nervously from the third-base line as his oldest grandson stepped up to bat.

I felt his eyes on me and the weight of my past and future baseball career as the echoes of Coach Brock's "pep talk" rang in my mind.

---

5   I wouldn't recommend this form of leadership in today's day and age, but it definitely worked back in 1994!

With runners on first and third, I worked the count to my favor and on a two-ball, one-strike got the fastball I'd been waiting for. I hit my first home run of the season off the left-field scoreboard and rounding third, saw my grandfather grinning with undisguised pride. In one of my life's happiest moments, I gave him the home run ball after the game, something he remembered right up until he passed away just shy of his one hundred-and-first birthday.

We ended up losing the game, but it turned out to be the turning point not only for me but for the team as well. We went on to finish third in the College World Series. Coach Brock's approach on that early morning in Tallahassee wouldn't fly with our HR manager today (nor should it), but the man was fearless and inspiring. It was an honor to play for him, and I'm forever grateful for the lessons in courage and leadership he taught me.

Early in my career, I let imposter syndrome (the fear of not having earned my spot) overshadow past accomplishments. Later, the lucky curse (the fear of not living up to my good fortune) let the weight of the world's expectations slow me down. At Arizona State, I finally realized what was at the core of all this negativity, and it was transformational for me.

It can be for you as well.

FEAR

No matter how it manifests (and it can be very inventive), fear is the thing most likely to keep people from achieving the great lives they want and deserve. Facing your fears involves learning about yourself. You need to understand the contexts that trigger them and what *exactly* it is that frightens you. Do you get anxious whenever you need to give a presentation or speak in front of a group? Are you afraid to have hard conversations? Are you secretly worried you're just not good enough?

Once you've identified what scares you, you can get to work overcoming it. I have a few tools I've collected over the years that I've found helpful in wrestling with self-doubt and anxiety: putting things in perspective, pushing the extreme, and (of course) learning.

PERSPECTIVE

When I find myself sweating the small stuff, I'll often bring to mind the way Coach Brock faced disease and death, and I'll take inspiration and courage from the way he faced much larger challenges. This isn't to diminish my situation or to trick myself into thinking that my own fears are illegitimate. The key is to find the strength to conquer your fear, not pretend that it isn't real. Perspective helps you do that by reminding you that people are remarkably strong and face much more challenging situations with courage. You can too.

PURPOSEFUL AWFULIZING

If you let it get away from you, imagining everything that can go wrong in a situation only feeds your fear, but sometimes it's all the unknowns that paralyze you. Ask yourself: *What would happen if your presentation doesn't go well? What happens if you get hung up on when you're making a sales call? What happens if an employee quits in the middle of a big project?*

Odds are, whatever the worst-case scenario is, it isn't as bad as your vague fears make it out to be. Most things are survivable. They may not always be comfortable, but you can handle discomfort. Life will go on after the presentation or sales call. And simply having survived it will help you build up resilience. (More about resilience in Chapter 3.)

LEARN IT!

Often an ignored but bubbling anxiety is your mind's way of letting you know you're not as prepared as you could be. Maybe you need to take a class on public speaking (I can recommend one!). Or maybe you struggle to book meetings on prospecting calls. Try setting up a time with your coworkers to roleplay whatever is making you anxious. Work it until your confidence is built back up, then get out there and make the calls or give that talk. What do you have to lose? Nothing!

You can never be fully prepared for everything, but the more prepared you are for any situation you're feeling unsure about, the more confident you'll feel. And while confidence isn't the antithesis of fear, it's a powerful damper. Experience helps too. The more frequently you face your fears and do what scares you, the easier it gets. The fear of making prospecting calls never goes away completely, but the more you get out of your comfort zone and do the work, the easier and better at it you get.

The simple act of naming a fear helps bring it under control. It also gives you the chance to deliberately try out some tricks for managing it. And managing your fear frees your imagination to do something more inspiring.

HAVE A VISION

Growing up, I was lucky to have my father as an example. Walt Lembi

("Big W" as my friends called him) had a real gift for coming up with grand ideas and exploring them to their fullest. He tried a lot of things. Some of them failed, but it never stopped him from trying again. It was from him that I learned about moon shot thinking and going after the big idea.

Don't be afraid to set your goals high. If you have a vision of increasing the value of your business from $5 million to $100 million and fall short by half, hey you still hit $50 million! There's nothing wrong with dreaming big. If you're leading a $10 million division or company, aspire to make it a $100 million one. If you don't set stretch goals, you will never reach your full potential. Like Les Brown famously said, "Shoot for the moon and if you miss, you'll land in the stars."

Vision differentiates leaders from operators. Operators work toward an organization's goal and are vital to its smooth functioning, but they don't set the agenda. Leaders avoid getting stuck in operator mode by using their energy to focus on what's ahead. Walt Lembi was a visionary and a leader. He set lofty goals and went all in. Some- times his risk-taking and boldness rubbed people the wrong way, but he never got mired in the minutiae.

Setting lofty goals is important for you as a leader, but it's also important to encourage the people you lead to do the same. When a team member comes to me with a big idea, I might not always think it's feasible, but I don't share my skepticism with them. Instead I start working with them on how to get there. I encourage their vision and give them the opportunity to create a strategy and try for their goal. You almost have to go against your first instincts when you're assessing big goals. It can be a huge positive to allow your vision to be stretched beyond what you once thought possible, and that's a gift you can give the people on your team too.

My dad also taught me the motivational power of having a big, even outrageous, vision. When I was a kid, he'd come to my basketball or soccer games and deliver amazing speeches. They never failed to get everybody pumped up. Even if we were the underdog team facing an undefeated one, Big W would find a way to inspire us to get out there and win. He knew vision lit people's fire. Once when I was about ten, I was playing in a soccer tournament and my dad, of course, was there to watch. We won the morning game, which meant we'd play another after lunch. We were more tired than excited. He loaded the entire team into our Toyota van and took us to a matinee of *The Karate Kid*. It did exactly what he must have known it would. We saw ourselves in Daniel and Mr. Miyagi's story, and we crushed our afternoon opponents.

My dad's power to inspire wasn't about his eloquence or the specific words he said, it was about his passion and delivery. He might say something as simple as, "Let's make this happen!" But his confidence that we *could* make it happen and the energy he brought to that conviction told us, even as little kids, that his belief in us was authentic. Demonstrate the same enthusiastic confidence in your people when they come to you with a big idea. If you don't show that you're willing to believe in their vision, they'll quickly lose their own confidence in it.

Developing a vision doesn't come easy for most people. Fortunately for those of us who aren't born visionaries like Steve Jobs or Elon Musk, there are frameworks that can help guide the process.

My "go-to" framework for developing and enhancing my company vision is Vision Scripter, which helps you describe your company's future reality as if it was happening in the present.[6] You can then

---

6   The Vision Scripter exercise comes from Michael Hyatt's great book, *The Vision Driven Leader: 10 Questions to Focus Your Efforts, Energize Your Team, and Scale Your Business* (Grand Rapids: Baker Books, 2020).

make that vision into reality by breaking it into goals, helping your people focus on them, and providing feedback to keep them on track.

GOALS

When you have a big vision, it's easy to get intimidated by its scope, scale, and ambition. Break your vision into big goals and your big goals into smaller, bite-sized ones that feel more attainable. I recommend having a few big yearly goals that inspire you as well as monthly, weekly, and daily goals that you know you can reach. These smaller goals serve as a roadmap to your eventual destination, improve your discipline, and keep you focused on what to do next. Importantly, they also set up small wins along the way that reinforce your confidence and boost your energy. Don't forget to celebrate them!

Limit the number of yearly goals you have. You can't accomplish everything, and paring down your goals allows you to focus on the most important. My recommendation is to set between three and five annual goals. To greatly improve your chance of good outcomes, divide these ambitious year goals into three or four small milestones or goals you'll focus on for each of the year's quarters. Creating these smaller goals shows you the entire process without overwhelming you. Then prioritize your time and focus on achieving those quarterly goals.[7]

Write your goals down and share them with others. People who share their goals are more likely to keep their commitments. This applies to personal goals and professional goals. I share my own goals with my team—my goals for the quarter, but also some of my personal ones. When you're vulnerable enough to share your plans

---

[7]   I even take the process a step further. I plan out weekly goals that tie back to my quarterly goals and then focus daily on achieving my weekly goals, which roll up to quarterly and then yearly ones.

in detail, you feel the community behind you, helping hold you accountable. Demonstrating your commitment to goals and goal-setting can also inspire and influence the people you lead.

FOCUS

Having clear goals clearly linked to an inspiring vision creates focus. When you have a clear sense of what you're trying to accomplish and why, you can see what needs your attention and find the motivation to focus on it. Whether you're preparing for a presentation or a big game, if you know you've put in the work ahead of time, you can step up to the plate or podium with confidence. Whatever fear or anxiety you might be feeling, shift your focus to what you've already accomplished. Remind yourself that you've done the work to earn success, then trust the mechanics you've honed through practice. Then relax and focus on the task at hand.

The same is true of your team. Often what looks like a lack of performance is a lack of focus which, in turn, comes from a lack of clarity. Create dedicated time and space to check in on your team's progress. If they aren't moving toward their goals with energy and focus, make sure they're all in. If they're not, is fear getting in their way? Offer perspective and reassure them. I've found I need to constantly remind my people that failure *is* an option—and sometimes a good one! If they're working with focus toward a goal that serves our shared vision, they aren't going to get in trouble with me for failing to reach it. I'd rather see them run and fall than amble along safely just doing the bare minimum.

If a team member is underperforming and fear isn't the reason, make sure they understand and believe in the purpose behind the company's vision (or as it's often called, its "why"). Sometimes a lack of clarity is the reason for a lack of focus. If people don't understand the why of their goals and how those goals serve the larger purpose, they can miss out on the energy that comes from working toward the company's inspiring vision.

If they're not clear on how what they do serves the organization and its vision, ask questions and listen to what they have to say. Help your people understand the impact of the contribution only they can make. If they do understand the why behind their goals, and they're still not focused on reaching them, it may be time to have a difficult conversation.

FEEDBACK

Delivering feedback about an employee's performance isn't always comfortable, but if you show that you're committed not only to the vision and goals of the company but also to their individual growth, you build trust and create a relationship where everyone is focused on the task at hand.

For feedback to be most effective, it needs to be a two-way street. Good leaders don't take criticism personally or worry about making people like them. Concentrating on what others think of you is fear-based thinking that can keep you from going all in. It's wonderful to be liked, but if you put your own image or need for approval ahead of the needs of your team and your company, it will be that much harder to get where you want to go. When you solicit constructive criticism, avoid the temptation to become defensive or offer excuses. Instead think of how you can use the criticism productively.

From Adam Grant's fabulous book *Think Again: The Power of Knowing What You Don't Know*, I learned a great tip on how to invite feedback from people who report to you and others who might be reluctant to speak openly and honestly. In a particularly relevant example, I sent the first draft of this manuscript to Jose Castro, a trusted friend who was one of Learnit's all-time great leaders for over twenty years. I asked him, "Would you mind reading through Chapter 7 for me? I'm not sure I am a fan of the section 'Learning to Inspire.'" By addressing Jose this way, I showed my vulnerability and openness to not being perfect. In my experience, this opens the door to eliciting better and more legitimate feedback. It certainly did this book some good!

Great feedback can come from all levels of your organization. Frontline workers, for example, are often in the best position to know what customers need. Encourage all of your team members to give you feedback honestly and openly by regularly making yourself available for them to come talk to you and by being present and attentive when they do. There may be no better way to demonstrate what vision and goal-directed focus look like. Focus on what is being said. Be a good listener. After all, listening is how we learn.

LISTENING

Go all in when you listen. I see a lot of leaders get this wrong by attempting to multitask during a meeting or, even worse, glancing at social media while someone is talking. Model the focus you want to see in your people. They won't be inspired to come up with new ideas or motivated to work their hardest for you if you're unfocused or distracted. Allowing your attention to drift breaks down trust, undermines confidence, and sets a bad example.

A GOOD LEADER IS AN EXCELLENT LISTENER.

To be a good listener, you first must hear what people are saying. Don't start formulating a response in your mind while you pretend to be giving your full attention. Just listen. Make whoever is talking to you feel like the most important person in the room. The more focused your attention, the better you'll be able to pose questions that dig deeply into the specific task you and your team are trying to accomplish together. It's hard to ask good questions if your mind is on the next meeting, and it's the answers to these thoughtful questions that will improve your own learning.

CHAPTER SUMMARY

Learn-it-all leaders learn to handle fear by going all in on learning. When you're fully and passionately committed to learning, failure becomes impossible. If you believe that no matter what happens you'll have learned something valuable, fear can no longer stop you. Having learned to be fearless, learn-it-all leaders are free to dream bolder dreams and advocate for an inspiring vision for both their company as a whole and the individual members of its teams.

They break their vision down into goals and milestones, providing clarity and focus for themselves and their teams. They're more able than know-it-alls to be present in the moment and attentive to the people and the learning opportunities each situation presents. Putting moment-to-moment focus all in on learning, coupled with a vision for the future and a learner's agenda, allows them to bounce back even when things don't work out the way they'd hoped.

My baseball career may not have worked out the way I envisioned it would, but I am grateful for the lessons I learned, especially from the amazing coaches I had. I applied these learnings and experiences at my first "real job," where I started on the lowest rung of the ladder.

CHAPTER 2

ASSUME NOTHING

I'll tell the story of how (and why) my dad started Learnit in the next chapter, but he was just getting it up and running as my college and baseball careers were winding down. Even though I didn't have any real-world business experience, he knew I was a hard worker, a fast learner, and competitive. I was grateful that he was willing to give me an opportunity, but I knew I would have to prove myself.

I started at Learnit the day we opened in June of 1995 as a receptionist, answering phones, and helping out wherever I could. I came in humble, eager to learn and prove my worth. I did whatever I was asked to—I taught classes, hit the phones and made cold calls, and even helped out with the IT work. It was a tremendous learning experience. For over four years, I worked hard, striving to prove my value, and I sincerely enjoyed the opportunity to learn and grow.

As the company headed into its fifth year, our CEO, John Ashton, decided he was ready to move on. When the Learnit board started the process of finding a successor, I asked to be considered for the position. During the interview process, I was able to explain why

I felt I could leverage my experience to help drive Learnit toward its goals. I earned the board's confidence and was rewarded with the opportunity to become the new CEO. Five years into my professional career, I was at the helm of Learnit and needed to lean into learning everything I could to prove to the board—but more importantly to my father—that they had made the right choice!

BE HUMBLE

The humble learn-it-all knows they don't know it all. They're not too proud to seek out (and take!) input and advice from others. They consciously practice keeping a beginner's mind and work on developing a growth mindset. They're able to admit when they're off course and do what's necessary to get back on track.

ADVICE

My dad was a huge sports fan and an "out of the box thinker" (or crazy scheme guy, depending on your perspective). One day in 1997, he came into the Learnit offices with the Bay Area sportscasting legend Mark Ibanez, and an idea only Big W could have dreamed up.

It went this way: Mark would cold call companies and say, "Hi, this is Mark Ibanez from Channel Two Sports. I'm involved with this great company called Learnit and I'd like to set up a meeting with you to learn more about how you are handling computer training at your company."

HR managers were surprised to hear Mark's familiar voice on their voicemail and it was amazing how many doors to customer meetings it opened for us.

One of the callbacks Mark got was from Tarina Hall, the Head of Learning and Development at Gap Inc. Tarina told Mark that his timing was perfect; she and her team were about to open up an RFP (request for proposal) on computer training for their corporate staff. At the time, Learnit didn't have any customers even a fraction of that size, and I still vividly remember walking with Mark into the Gap Inc.'s headquarters more nervous than I'd been since the College World Series.

Over the following weeks, we had several great meetings with Tarina and her team. I could tell they liked our energy and the potential opportunity to be a very big fish in our smaller pond. They could anticipate the level of personal attention they would receive from Learnit as our flagship client. Their biggest concern was that Learnit might be too small to handle an account of their magnitude. Did we have enough classrooms? How many instructors did we have to fulfill their requests? Could Learnit handle training initiatives for Gap offices throughout the country?

They were valid questions and to be honest, I wasn't sure I had the answers. But I'd learned early on that a leader doesn't need to. If you surround yourself with smart people and can tap into your extended network for advice, you can learn what you need to.

My dad wasn't involved in the day-to-day at Learnit but he was always curious about what we had going on and who our customers were. He was also kind enough to frequently take me along on his own business trips as he conducted our family real estate business. Being able to accompany my dad on these trips and absorb everything was an incredible learning experience. Sitting in on those meetings, often as the proverbial fly on the wall, watching Big W impress Ivy League bankers from the largest firms in the world always made me proud of my dad. It also taught me the importance of storytelling, speaking with confidence, and anticipating questions.

I took one of these trips in the middle of our battle to win Gap Inc. My dad was meeting with Spencer Young who, at the time, ran Morgan Stanley's commercial mortgage-backed securities division. Spencer was a big-time guy engaged in his own battle to win our family's billion-dollar real estate business against competition from the likes of UBS and Lehman Brothers. I didn't say much during the meeting but as we were leaving the conference for lunch, my dad turned to Spencer and said, "Hey Spencer, my kid has a huge opportunity to win Gap Inc.'s computer training business. What advice can you give him?"

Standing in the hallway of Morgan Stanley on the forty-fifth floor, looking out over the Hudson River, we were suddenly talking about Learnit. Spencer was caught a little off guard, but he regrouped quickly. "Okay Damon," he said. "Tell me more."

I gave him the two-minute summary.

"Got it," he said. "They like your company but they're concerned about going with Learnit instead of one of the national players in your space. It's a common challenge for new businesses. Here's what you do: every time you call your contacts at Gap Inc., add value. Don't waste their time calling just to check in.

"Always speak with confidence and end every conversation by telling them that, if given the opportunity, your team will exceed their expectations. And then do just that. Exceed expectations they don't know they have. Find a way to be unique. Learn everything you can about their culture and their business goals. Then paint them the picture of how Learnit will help them reach those goals and what accomplishing them will look like. Do it with confidence and believe it yourself. They won't believe you can do it if you don't. Damon, they want a training partner who has the necessary confidence to make this partnership work. Show them you've got it."

I took Spencer's advice and acted on it, pulling out all the stops to win the contract. It worked.

I sent Spencer a note right after we got the great news. I told him how I'd incorporated his advice into our winning strategy, and I thanked him for his help. People like to help. And they love it when they know their advice has been taken and appreciated.

ASK FOR ADVICE. ACT ON IT. SHARE YOUR RESULTS AND SAY THANK YOU.

COACHING

Learn-it-alls don't just take great advice when it's offered. They actively seek out coaches and mentors to advise them and reinforce the fundamentals throughout their careers. The greats in sports understand this concept. Even at the heights of their careers, Michael Jordan and Tiger Woods still had coaches because they knew that there was always something that they could improve on. I'm a big believer in executive coaching and still have a coach myself.

A good coach will find ways to stretch your skills and force you out of your comfort zone. The greatest coaches, like the greatest leaders, provide quality, critical feedback. Have the humility to both seek that out and accept it. No matter how high you rise, stay coachable.

Confidence is great, but people who are confident they "know it all" can miss learning opportunities out of sheer pride. I once hired a new salesperson who'd recently graduated from a top university. In advance of his first large-scale opportunity, I asked him to include one of our senior sales executives on an upcoming customer call to support him. When I followed up a couple of days later to ask how the call went and whether the senior sales executive had been helpful, his reply was, "You know, I thought about it, but I didn't need her on the call. I was confident I could handle it on my own."

We lost the deal.

I am not saying that having the senior executive accompany him would have guaranteed a win, but what I can tell you is it wouldn't have hurt. Without a doubt, she would have been able to assist the new hire and provide post-call constructive feedback that would have helped him throughout his career.

I set aside time to speak to the young man and shared with him how important it is to take advantage of such opportunities to have more experienced team members support him with prospects and, more importantly, with his professional growth. I also pointed out that I hadn't asked him if he *wanted* to have her attend the meeting. I'd asked him to have her there. It hadn't been optional.

Maybe it was the pride of a young man eager to prove he could do it on his own, but someone with a learn-it-all mindset realizes that having a team member help takes nothing away from your individual accomplishment. It just gives you a better chance of winning the deal. Take pride in your wins *and* your coachability, not in having gone it alone. Or, as Laurel Taylor, an incredible leader in her own right (who started her career at Learnit and is now the founder and CEO of Futurefuel.io) told me years ago, "I learned to put pride aside and not be afraid to accept help when it's available. At the end of the day, it's all about results and learning. Don't let ego stop you from taking advantage of people's generosity."

BEGINNER'S MIND

In an interesting paradox, humility requires confidence. Admitting that you don't immediately know the correct approach to a problem makes you vulnerable—something people lacking in confidence are often unwilling to do. Part of a leader's job is to create an environment of trust where people feel safe enough to be vulnerable. (More on creating a learn-it-all culture in Chapter 6.) Importantly, you, as the leader, have to be able to trust the people you work with too so you can be vulnerable enough to bring a beginner's mind to the table. You also need confidence in your ability to find your way through a problem without using preconceived notions as a crutch along the way.

> *THINKING LIKE A BEGINNER REQUIRES THE CONFIDENCE TO KEEP YOURSELF OPEN AND VULNERABLE.*

In trying to access a beginner's mind, it can help to think back to when you were a child and everything you experienced was new and unknown. In general, children experiment and observe. They don't have preconceived notions, and as a result, they can learn about the world rapidly. They're not afraid to make mistakes. They know that's the way we learn. As we get older, we tend to get more cautious, worrying about what people think of us. We become closed instead of remaining open to possibilities and learning, and that's a mistake.

It's easy, especially after a bit of success, to see yourself as an expert, and to feel as if you have arrived. But a leader who "knows it all" is just going to revert to old methods instead of testing new approaches or asking for input from quality team members.

It takes deliberate choices and effort to retain your beginner's mind. Early wins too easily lead to self-satisfaction, which all but inevitably leads to stagnation.

GROWTH MINDSET

Like maintaining your ability to access a beginner's mind, having a growth mindset[8] (in contrast to a fixed mindset) requires deliberate effort. It means putting your faith in effort over talent and attributing your good outcomes to hard work more than to innate ability. With a growth mindset, rather than letting undesirable outcomes become an indictment of your intelligence, your abilities, or of you as a person, you interpret failures and setbacks as a call to put in more or better practice. It's a little tricky to spot, but this way of framing bad outcomes is a form of humility too. You take responsibility for your mistakes or failures but you don't make them about you.

A good leader has the humility to say, "I made a mistake," and then analyze that mistake to learn from it in order to do a better job next time. It can be difficult to admit when you've been wrong, but it's important to develop a thick skin and to understand that mistakes are inevitable. This approach is far superior to becoming defensive and blaming others.

---

8   In her powerful book, *Mindset*, Carol Dweck, an expert and researcher in human motivation, defines a growth mindset as one based on the belief that intelligence, personality, and other traits can be deliberately cultivated.

COURSE CORRECTION

I've seen too many people cling to disproven plans and outdated dreams. Often they feel unfairly treated by an unexpected turn of events, and that sense of injustice keeps them from moving on. Certain individuals seem to always play the victim. Chances are, their ego is preventing them from being honest with themselves about the role they played in an outcome they don't like. As a result, they don't learn from their disappointments, improve, or achieve larger goals.

I love the quote, often attributed to John Maynard Keynes, "When events change, I change my mind. What do you do?"[9] It's much better to change your mind, your plans, and your answers whenever you realize reality or the facts aren't unfolding accordingly. Reality is a much tougher thing to alter. Switching gears is totally acceptable when you have confidence in your larger vision. Don't let your pride get in the way. Instead ask yourself: "What is the end goal?" If there's a better way to reach that goal by changing direction, make it happen, learn from your missteps, reflect on what you could have done differently or what changed, and move on.

Humility also allows you to spot when it's time to try something new. Even after you've made the decision to go all in on a project or career choice, things can go wrong. When they do, have the humility to recognize the situation for what it is—an opportunity to learn and pivot. Even after I went all in on pursuing a career in major league baseball, when it didn't work out the way I wanted it to, I let it go. I moved on and didn't dwell on the past. I had an incredible run and great lifelong friends, and I learned invaluable leadership lessons. It's hard to give up on a dream or even on a failing, multimillion-dollar project, but you need to avoid the sunk cost fallacy (the name econ-

9   The fascinating website QuoteInvestigator.com credits the less well-known Nobel-winning economist Paul Samuelson with the remark: https://quoteinvestigator.com/2011/07/22/keynes-change-mind/.

omists give to what Dad would have called "throwing good money after bad"). Lick your wounds and move on!

CHAPTER SUMMARY

Even if you're committed and have gone all in, you'll never be a great leader if you're arrogant or naive enough to think you have it all figured out. Trust me, you don't. Humility, openness to good advice and coaching, a beginner's mind, a growth mindset, and the ability to course-correct are your ticket to becoming a learn-it-all leader, even if none of us can ever learn it all.

Commitment and humility aren't enough to get you there. You also need to be deeply curious.

CHAPTER 3

WONDER WHY

Curiosity is the foundation of Learnit, and not just because it's the primary reason leaders and teams come to us to learn it—no matter what *it* is. The entire enterprise began when my father got curious about whether computer training had to be boring. It was 1993, and he'd recently bought his first Macintosh to keep track of his real estate portfolio electronically. He wasn't having much luck getting Excel to work for him, so he bought training classes for himself and my sisters at Comp USA.

Within the first hour of sitting in a sterile environment listening to a listless instructor read from a manual, Big thought to himself, "There has got to be a better way." Personal computers were still rather novel at that time—the wave of the future—and he thought learning to use them should be exciting. But he was bored. The environment was overly corporate. Famous for his short attention span, there was no way he was going to make it to the end of the day. At the lunch break, he turned to my sister Chelsea and delivered one of his famous lines: "Chels, take a picture of this place because you won't see me here again!"

None of them went back for the afternoon training but the experience sparked my dad's curiosity. Besides, he still wanted to learn how to organize his real estate portfolio electronically, so he did what great entrepreneurs tend to do. He created a scalable solution to a challenge he was experiencing. My dad figured (rightly, as it turned out) that there would soon be a need for more engaging corporate training to help close the skill gap the workforce was experiencing between the old and new tech. He started wondering how he could make computer training exciting and interactive. After mulling it over for a few days, he called up John Ashton, the former CFO at our family's savings and loan. "Hey John, I have a great idea!" he announced. "I want to launch a computer training company. You're the only person I know who gets computers. Let's make it happen!"

In typical Walt Lembi fashion, he took John to lunch and got him all pumped about his vision of building the best computer training company in the world. They'd offer computer classes that weren't boring or held in an office that looked like a hospital. "Classes should be short—no longer than ninety minutes—and affordable to everyone including college kids or career changers. And fun! We'll get actors, magicians, even comedians to teach them."

Another significant piece of the puzzle was the training location. He envisioned designing it to facilitate community and be a place where people would want to hang out. Essentially, he wanted to create the exact opposite of the computer store's sterile, tedious environment. "And," he told John, "I have the perfect person to design out the space—Linda!" (He was referring to his wife, my mom, who is a phenomenal interior designer and whose work at Learnit was instrumental to its success.) "I've got the perfect name too," he added. "Learnit. Whatever *it* is, people can learn it from us.

We'll start with computer training today, but who knows? Maybe next we'll do leadership training or foreign languages."

BE CURIOUS

If it weren't for my father's curiosity about creating a better way to deliver computer training, Learnit would never have gotten off the ground. In fact, curiosity might just be the foundational trait of the learn-it-all leader. A curious mind spots opportunities others might miss, improves decision-making, and promotes flexible thinking. Great leaders hire for this trait and create a culture of curiosity to foster teamwork, encourage transparency, improve performance, and deliver a superior customer experience.

POSSIBILITY SPOTTING

Curiosity allows you to view obstacles as interesting puzzles to solve rather than setbacks to passively endure. In the first months of 2020, as the pandemic started to slam the breaks on the economy, I was walking down the hill from my house listening to a Pat Lencioni podcast. In the episode "Plant Your Friggin Tree," he posed an important question: "Should we simply freeze and do nothing and wait for the pandemic to end? Or should we look around and see if we can turn some of the disadvantages into advantages?"[10]

Being a sports guy, I particularly loved an analogy he made to NBA players. They, he pointed out, could sit on the couch watching TV and grousing that their season had been canceled. Or they could

---

10   Patrick Lencioni, "48. Plant Your Friggin Tree," July 2020, in *At the Table with Patrick Lencioni*, podcast, 19:52, https://www.tablegroup.com/48-plant-your-friggin-tree/.

find an empty gym nearby, work on their free throws, and get ahead. His observations made me curious. What could Learnit do to take advantage of the awful situation instead of sitting there and letting it get the best of us?

I started to wonder what might be possible. With the world learning to adapt to virtual doctor's appointments and 100 percent remote work for most, was there an opportunity for Learnit to scale and expand our customer base with virtual instructor-led training? Instead of merely trying to survive, I wanted to dig deep and find a way to gain an advantage. I wanted us to help more organizations learn skills like adaptability, leading distributed teams, and running virtual meetings—skills that, overnight, were becoming mission-critical for organizations worldwide.

To accomplish that, we would need to do exactly what Pat had recommended in his podcast and the direct opposite of what the majority of the world was doing. Rather than cutting back, we'd need to increase our investment in our sales team. It was, after all, a great opportunity to find the kind of top-tier sales talent that's in prohibitively high demand in a tight market. I considered which careers might be most affected by the steadily increasing closures and landed on event planners and sales executives who sold luxury boxes at sporting events.

But before I went all in on my new idea, I sought advice, this time from my most loyal and reliable source. I am incredibly lucky to have a wife (Cara Mia Lembi) who has always been there to listen to my work trials and tribulations. Like any great partner, she's supportive but not shy. She's always willing to give me her unfiltered opinions and recommendations—solicited or not! In this particular situation, I sought out Cara's input because we'd be investing heavily at a time of enormous uncertainty and if I was wrong, it could have a potentially devastating impact on Learnit's future, on our family finances, and those of all the other families who relied on Learnit for their incomes.

Our conversation reminded me of the movie *Rocky II*. In the movie, Rocky's insane commitment to his rematch against Apollo Creed has forced Adrianne, his pregnant wife, to take a second job that endangers her health. In my all-time favorite scene, she wakes up from a coma to find Rocky by her side. He croaks out something like, "You know Adrianne, I don't have to fight Apollo again. I can give up boxing and find something else." Adrianne barely manages to whisper, "Win."

"What?" he asks.

"Rocky, do one thing for me—win!"

Now I know this is pretty cheesy (still, go back and watch this scene if you ever need to feel inspired), and my conversation with Cara wasn't nearly as dramatic. I told her about my plan to go all in and increase our sales team by 30 percent, and I laid out the potential risks. Without hesitating, she said, "Great idea. Go with your instincts. You got this!"

I left that conversation feeling like I could take on Apollo myself! Instead I jumped online, sent out over a hundred LinkedIn messages, and reached out to my network for referrals, letting everyone know we were looking for sales talent and were open to recruiting outside the Bay Area.

At first, some of our team members worried it was too risky to ramp up hiring during a pandemic, but it was a calculated risk, one I was willing to take. Luckily, it paid off. Our combined recruiting efforts resulted in seven new hires from across the country—five of whom are still with us today (and crushing it).

The pandemic allowed Learnit to expand our reach and add tremendous depth to our already strong sales team. All of our pandemic hires are great people and an enormous asset, and we wouldn't have them if I hadn't actively gone looking. My curiosity about who was being most negatively affected by the pandemic allowed us to make huge gains despite the tragic and chaotic times.

I took the same position of wondering about how negatives might make positives possible relative to our clients. With everyone stuck at home and getting used to conducting meetings online, I got curious again. How could we help our customers transition all their previously booked in-person training to virtual classes while ensuring comparable, if not superior outcomes? Was there an opportunity for companies to leverage our classes to create social engagement and encourage their employees to connect and bond in new ways? Could we create a sense of stability for our customers and help them be productive amid all the change, chaos, and fear?

Turns out, the answer was "yes" all around. I would never say COVID-19 was a good thing, but getting curious about how to approach the new normal allowed Learnit to face what was in front of us and pivot to meet emergent needs. We went possibility-spotting in those uncertain days and found opportunities for growth which helped our team and our customers pull through. Curiosity helped us build our talent pool and move forward in ways that would have been impossible had we not tackled the challenges head-on with an eye toward finding innovative solutions.

My advice for learning how to become better at possibility-spotting is threefold:

1. **Be adaptable and open to change.** Understand that "But this is how we have always done things" isn't a winning answer in our lightning-fast world. Being adaptable means quickly accepting the new reality is real and actively scouting for its equally new possibilities.

2. **Don't reinvent the wheel.** When we go looking for ways to evolve and grow Learnit, I encourage my team (and myself) to look beyond market trends, what our competitors are doing, and the latest fads in L&D. I encourage us all to look in alternative directions by asking questions like: What can we learn from Netflix and its customer-recommendation algorithms? What could we incorporate from JetBlue's approach that could enhance Learnit's customer experience? By looking outside our industry and stretching our imaginations to see how innovations elsewhere might guide change here, we've been able to see possibilities others have missed.[11]

3. **Diversify your team.** A diverse team brings unique points of view to the table which, if you keep an open mind, can open up an endless stream of possibilities. We'll talk more about diversity in Chapter 6, but it isn't limited to race and gender. Include people of different ages and levels of experience. You'll be surprised how much having a range of experience contributes to creative problem-solving.

DECISION-MAKING

Leaders often have a gut-level sense of how to make decisions, but I've found it's vital to stay curious and ask questions. I'm interested

---

11 A great quick read on the subject is the book *Steal Like an Artist: 10 Things Nobody Told You About Being Creative* by Austin Kleon.

in what other people are thinking—especially when they express a different view I haven't heard or don't find immediately intuitive. The right questions, asked with genuine curiosity, can change the balance of a crucial decision.

We'll talk more about how to make good decisions in Chapter 5, but curiosity plays a key role in the input-getting phase. Resist the temptation of thinking, "It's my way or the highway." According to a study in the journal *Natural Human Behaviour*, researchers at Caltech determined that somewhere between eight and fifteen choices significantly improves your odds of making a good decision, so get additional input.[12] Try to withhold judgment as you listen to the ideas of others, stay present, and truly pay attention to all points of view, especially opposing ones. This gets more important the more experienced and convinced of your own opinion you are. By staying open and curious, you're giving yourself more options.

When I look back at earlier points in my career, I can see times when I had a closed mind or when I was defensive in the face of others' opinions. Now I'm more curious about differing viewpoints and seek them out—and not only from senior leaders. Frontline workers are a gold mine of information. In several instances, what I've learned by seeking out the insight of those closest to our customers has proved invaluable and led to better decisions. Tom Peters in his management classic, *In Search of Excellence,* calls this "management by wandering around" (MBWA). I believe letting your curiosity drive you out of your office and into conversations with team members of all levels (in-person or virtually) is vital to becoming a learn-it-all leader.

---

12   Elena Reutskaja et al., "Choice Overload Reduces Neural Signatures of Choice Set Value in Dorsal Striatum and Anterior Cingulate Cortex," *Nature Human Behaviour* 2 (2018): 925–935, https://www.nature.com/articles/s41562-018-0440-2.

Making big decisions well is both art *and* science and needs both logical and creative thinking. Look for additional options, think out of the box, and trust your intuition but make sure you also understand the facts. For critically important decisions (e.g., whether to leave your current company or relocate your family), dig deep. Use your imagination to think through worst and best-case scenarios and develop rational contingencies.

GREAT LEADERS ARE
GREAT DECISION-MAKERS.

If you aspire to be a learn-it-all leader, I recommend getting into the habit of carving out time to get curious specifically about the art and science of decision-making. There are hundreds of books, blogs, and podcasts on the topic. My top go-to resources are:

- *The Farnam Street* podcast and blog. Shane Parrish and his team share great insights on mental models and how to make smarter decisions.
- Daniel Kahneman. Known for his classic book, *Thinking Fast and Slow*, Kahneman is considered the godfather of judgment and decision-making. I'm always on the lookout for articles, books, and podcasts he's contributed to.
- Biographies. Reading biographies allows you to learn from the most famously successful (and biggest failures) in history. Biographies capture decades of experience and give you a "behind-the-scenes" look at some of the best and worst decisions ever made. My first recommendation to any new leader is to read ten to twenty biographies of leaders across the spectrum of areas of endeavor—from great innovators like Steve Jobs to world

leaders like Nelson Mandela, and from human rights activist Eleanor Roosevelt to wartime heroes like Winston Churchill.

FLEXIBLE THINKING

With the rapid changes happening now in the business world, it's vital for leaders to evolve quickly and nimbly adapt to the times. Maintaining a high level of curiosity as a lifelong learner allows you to keep your thinking flexible enough to respond to change well.

This trait, more formally called "learning agility," will be one of (if not the) most important skills in the workplace for the future.[13] The old-school business mindset was to hold a steady course in the face of change. The leaders of the past were confident and sure of themselves, and they had impressive accomplishments to prove that they knew what they were doing. But a lot of those same leaders failed when times changed. They were slow to adapt and dismissive of the new ideas people brought to them. It's important to rely on facts, but when facts change, you must be open to revisiting your decisions. If you can be humble and curious about the changes that are happening, then you will be flexible enough to seize opportunities when they arise.

I come from a family full of great business leaders, and I'm extraordinarily lucky to have such experience and knowledge guiding me and informing my own leadership style. All the same, I'm very aware that just because something worked for my father, grandfather, or brother Taylor doesn't mean it will work for me today. Staying curious helps keep me from falling into ruts and blindly following precedents.

---

13   Learning agility is defined as the ability to pick up new skills and apply them in your daily life. Specific to the workplace, it's how readily you upskill or reskill to continually progress your career.

The dangers of holding inflexibly to how things have always been done came into sharp focus for me during the pandemic. The transition from bustling offices to working from home was difficult for everyone, but even the most old-school companies had to adapt. Where I've seen their inflexibility become a sometimes crippling issue has been in how different leaders handled anticipating what would happen when employees returned to the office. Some companies, still stuck in a prepandemic frame of mind, forced people to come back before they were ready. Convinced that workers were less productive at home (despite strong evidence to the contrary), they insisted on "getting back to normal." I'm not sure "normal" is a thing that ever really existed and getting back to it is like trying to return to your childhood—the reality wouldn't match the memory. Besides, it's not really possible. To my mind, the Great Resignation we witnessed was a direct result of a lack of flexibility in leadership. Workers, fed up with jobs that refused to change, changed jobs, or simply refused them.

A leader who is curious about the changing needs of workers and flexible enough to meet them can easily recruit great talent simply by learning how hybrid models can be every bit as efficient as the old ways and even better than the old normal—whatever that was. A curious leader could have listened to employees in the first place and addressed their concerns rather than assuming that the world would simply return to the way it was before.

INFORMATION SEEKING

In order to truly serve your customers and differentiate your organization from your competitors, it's imperative you stay curious about what's going on in the world beyond your specific industry. Keeping yourself up-to-date on everything from the local economy to world affairs helps build your business acumen and contributes to more insightful and impactful discussions with customers (and friends!).

One of my favorite thought leaders in sales, Anthony Iannarino, highlights the advantages of information seeking in his book *Elite Sales Strategies*. Iannarino explains that a rigorous and ongoing search for knowledge enables you to provide your customers with new insights and creates an "information disparity" in your favor. I dedicate an hour every morning to keeping informed by either reading or watching the news while I exercise. CNBC's "Squawk Pod," the *Wall Street Journal*, the *New York Times*, the *Harvard Business Review*, and the local-to-me *San Francisco Business Times* are my go-to sources.

INTERESTED IS INTERESTING

Extend your curiosity to people as well. Take an active interest in your team members and learn about their hobbies, families, and interests outside of work. Not only will this create a strong professional bond, it will help you better understand the needs and motivations of the people you need to motivate. If you express interest in only their work and performance metrics, your employees may not feel you value them as individuals. But if they see you putting in a sincere effort to get to know them, sense that you understand they have lives and challenges outside of work, know you care, and believe you have their back, they'll feel individually valued. This creates a better work atmosphere and will often make people willing to extend themselves in return.

I like to end most conversations with my team members by asking, "Is there anything else you'd like to discuss?" in case there's something that hasn't come up but is on their minds. This open-ended question is designed to elicit anything that might be bothering them (work-related or not) that they'd like to address while they have my attention. Sometimes all it takes is a little space for people to surface what matters most.

You can also just pick up the phone (or these days jump on a Microsoft Teams call) and ask people how they're doing—a long-standing habit of mine—which I was touched to have one of our top instructors call out recently. In an internal training on leading hybrid teams, he told the group, "And you can just, you know, call your team members. Every now and again just out of the blue, Damon calls me to ask how my family is doing. I don't think he realizes how much it means to me that he does it, but it really helps me feel connected."

Not only will staying curious about your people improve the work environment, there's a strong business case for it as well. In July 2019, I sat down for a one-on-one with Carly Lutz, then one of our newest team members. She was very early on in her professional career, but she had the work ethic and learn-it-all attitude that made her an ideal addition to our team. I was curious about her experience as a new hire and was gratified that she felt comfortable enough with me to share her concerns. She said that while she loved Learnit's mission of helping individuals upskill and supporting companies in reaching their goals by developing their internal talent, she wasn't excited to come to work every day and hit the phones. She didn't enjoy outside sales as much as she'd thought she would. In fact, she was starting to dread it.

I took in this information and didn't get defensive (she'd only been on board for ninety days after all). Instead I got curious. I asked her if she thought there was a role that would be a better fit. She wasn't sure. I asked what excited her. Carly answered instantly. She said she was passionate about building community and networking with like-minded individuals. She'd heard tech companies were hiring community managers, which sounded very exciting to her and more in line with her self-perceived strengths than her current job in sales. Looking a little abashed, she confessed she'd been thinking about leaving Learnit and changing careers.

What Carly didn't know was that I'd dreamed for years of building an online community for our customers. I believed it would add significant value to our offerings if Learnit clients had a place to meet informally, learn from one another, and interact with our expert instructors beyond the classroom. I mentioned this to Carly and asked if she thought that was something she'd like to tackle. She lit up. She sat up straighter. I could feel the energy of her enthusiasm for the project like an electric current. "Absolutely," she said. "I would love to do that!" We decided she'd take two weeks and build out a high-level business plan to present to me and the Learnit executive team.

Carly blew us away with that presentation; her vision for the platform, her forecasts, timelines, and suggested strategies were spot on. She spelled out milestones to take us from the present to the launch of the online community, the KPIs (key performance indicators) to which we should hold her accountable, the amount of investment needed, and the potential risks associated with launching an online community. As I've told Carly several times since, her presentation reminded me of how Learnit won the Gap bid. It far exceeded expectations and radiated confidence. I was astonished by the sophistication of her strategic thinking, especially considering she was fewer than two years into her professional career. Carly was (and still is) a rock star. She spearheaded OFFSITE (a thriving online community) for Learnit. Even though she has moved on from

Learnit to follow her passions elsewhere, Carly is and always will be an important part of Learnit's history.

INTEREST AS INVESTMENT

Curiosity may be the single biggest driver in both revenue and the bottom line. Asking your customers thought-provoking and strategic questions helps them uncover unforeseen challenges that, once recognized, will allow you to work together on tackling them. Sure there are pain points and challenges that are clear and easy to see, such as trouble with employee retention or missing quarterly sales goals, but the ability to dig deeper and help your customers uncover underlying root causes they may not have spotted increases your value to them and differentiates you from the competition.

Let's take high attrition rates as an example. It's a problem that many organizations face and one we frequently discuss with clients. Often the business leaders we speak to think people are leaving their company for higher compensation or better perks at brand-name organizations. If, in reality, attrition is due to one of their manager's poor communication skills, spotting that can help us help them. The manager probably isn't intentionally letting down his direct reports; he may have been recently promoted without enough training in how to lead teams. If he isn't making his direct reports feel appreciated, they may be leaving to find managers at other companies who make them feel valued. This is a common and addressable challenge, but one you'll only surface if you get curious, ask the right questions, and really listen to your customers.

While Henry Ford probably didn't actually say that if he'd asked his customers what they needed, they would have said a faster horse, the idea behind the misattributed quote still stands. Customers don't always understand what they really need; it's your responsibility to guide them by getting curious and sharing your expertise. I've recommended the book *Questions are the Answer* by Hal B. Gregersen to dozens of leaders and have personally seen the proof of its thesis—to get better answers, ask better questions. This one skill returns your investment tenfold.

Curiosity can pay dividends even when you don't expect it. A story I've told at least a thousand times because it's one of my favorites involves my dad and part of his weekly routine. Every Monday night for years, my dad would park his Bentley at the Russ Street garage and walk across the street to meet me at the Learnit headquarters. We'd head over to Bob's Steakhouse at the Omni Hotel. (It's my version of Sam's bar from the 1980s TV show *Cheers*.)

As we were wrapping up dinner one night, my dad needed to jump on an important call. He asked me to retrieve his car from the garage and pick him up at the hotel. I was already late getting home, but how could I say no after another great dinner at Bob's? Besides, he always picked up the check! So I walked over into the Pine Street entrance and down to the garage where I was greeted by a chant of, "Learnit, Learnit!"

When I grinned at the three attendants, one of them asked, "Hey Damon, where's Mr. Walt?"

I explained the situation, and they pointed to the Bentley with its Learnit license plate parked, as always, in the front row. One of the attendants, an older man who was a staple of the Russ Street garage said, "Hey kid, you ever wonder why your father's car is always parked right here in front?"

I realized I hadn't and asked him about it.

"Out of all the people who park here, your dad is the only one who's at all interested in us. He's always asking how our families are doing, curious as to what's going on with our lives. He treats us like equals. That doesn't happen much around here with all these high-powered men and women. To most of them, it's like we don't even exist. But not Mr. Walt. He's a good guy with a big heart."

"Yeah," I agreed. "He really is."

The old guy grinned and gave me a wink. "Doesn't hurt that he's also a good tipper!"

We shared a laugh, and I got into the car, but he held onto the keys a minute longer. "You know he's proud of you, kid. And of Learnit. Always comes around telling us about the new customers you have and offering us free computer classes. Like I said, he's a good man and we all appreciate him. The way we park this car is how we show it."

It was a great lesson for me. Everyone from the CEO of a Fortune 100 company to the parking lot attendant has a story. You can learn something from anyone if you're curious about them. And that curiosity creates value for you and them. Seeing the impact my dad's simple interest in them made on the parking lot guys stuck with me. I still do my best to emulate Mr. Walt!

CHAPTER SUMMARY

Curiosity is where learning starts. When you engage with the world and wonder about why things are the way they are and how they could be better, you're able to spot opportunities that other, purely goal-directed people miss. Because curiosity leads you to ask more and better questions of more people, it opens you up to a diversity of perspectives and improves decision-making. It helps keep you agile, which allows you to adapt and change with the times rather than getting stuck in the past or in habitual ways of thinking and doing things.

My dad's sincere curiosity about the lives of everyone he came into contact with and his willingness to listen with interest taught me a valuable lesson: curiosity helps you learn but it also builds relationships inside a business and out. When you're genuinely curious about people, you recognize the humanity of everyone. You don't just talk to folks—you listen. And listening is what turns curiosity into learning (always a win for the learn-it-all leader!). It's also a win for everyone on those leaders' teams because it demonstrates respect for them, and respect—for yourself and others—is the core tenet of doing the right thing.

CHAPTER 4

DO THE RIGHT THING

My dad loved hiring his friends and family to work with him. Walt's buddies were (and still are) a bunch of characters, and I've done my best to emulate him on both counts—in hiring friends and family, but even more, in being a collector of interesting friends. One of his longest friendships was with Bert Strane, his college roommate at Santa Clara University. As a kid, I remember Bert coming over to the house in his flashy red shoes, taking me out to Washington Park, hitting ground balls, and throwing me batting practice. He and his twin brother Alvin were the star second baseman and shortstop for the Santa Clara Broncos baseball team in 1968, and both were drafted by the Los Angeles Dodgers later that year. When Bert's baseball career came to an end, he joined our family real estate company (Skyline Realty) and later became a mortgage broker for our Home Owner's Finance Company.

Walt and Bert were lifelong friends, but it's what Bert did at the end of my dad's life that made the strongest impression on me. In July of 2010, my dad was in the hospital, his battle with cancer coming to an end. Bert had been a frequent and loyal visitor, and one day, out of the blue, he said, "Hey Walt, you remember all the good we did for the kids in my old neighborhood back in the '80s? Let's do it again!"

Bert was talking about the outreach program for minority kids in the bay area that he and my dad created together. As an African American who'd come up without much in the way of privilege or opportunity, the mission was important to Bert. For Kids Opening Day at Candlestick Park on the second Saturday of the season in 1982, our savings and loan (Continental Savings and Loan) purchased 20,000 gameday tickets. It bussed in kids and their parents from all over the bay area, the majority of whom had never been to a pro sporting event. It even reserved 25 percent of Candlestick's parking lot to host a huge pregame BBQ. I was ten and got to be the Giants' honorary bat boy! I was scared to death sitting in the dugout with all my idols, but it was a great day.

All those years later, at his college roommate's bedside, Bert planned a reprise of the work they'd done and the good it had accomplished. He dreamed up Baseball for the Stars (which ran for seven consecutive years until Bert moved to Atlanta). "We can bring in current and ex-ball players to share their stories and show these young kids that their life has purpose and they can be winners too," he told my dad. "We'll all work together again to help kids through athletics, just like the old days."

My dad didn't recover, even with this great mission set out for him, and when he died, Bert doubled down on the idea, recasting it as a tribute. Knowing how important helping people had been to my dad, Bert thought it would make the best memorial to his spirit and generosity. I agreed. Together, he and I reached out to several former major league ballplayers we knew from our playing days. We got some big names including Rickey Henderson, Joe Morgan, Steve

Sax, Coco Crisp, Jacob Cruz, and even basketball star John Salley to come out to the field and speak with the kids, sharing their stories of failure, adversity, resilience, and larger goals.

My dad's relationships with Bert and with other business colleagues and family friends have had an enormous influence on me and on the type of relationships I strive to create personally and professionally. I have a strong commitment to living up to my father's example of treating everyone fairly even if sometimes that means helping them transition out of our company.

It's somewhat trendy to refer to your employees and yourself as a "family," but I've never really thought that was a good comparison. It's not that the people of Learnit and I aren't close—over the years, dozens of my team members have become lifelong friends—but "family" isn't quite the right way to describe the relationship. I think of us more as a team than a family. I know this could sound harsh, but think about it—you can't outgrow your family. Your parents will always be your parents. Your siblings will always be your siblings (even if you paint them red). The same isn't true of your employees. Sometimes even a great and loyal employee outgrows their role at a company. Sometimes a company's needs stretch beyond what a certain team member is capable of delivering. That's okay. Throughout the years, I've experienced this phenomenon several times and in the majority of them, people left the company as friends and loyal Learnit alumni.

Jim Mollé was an amazing instructor at Learnit for sixteen-plus years. He was instrumental in developing the direction of our Microsoft class curriculum and was a key team member in winning the Gap Inc. account all those years ago. Jim and I grew to be very close friends at work and outside of it. I'm even godfather to his eldest daughter. So when it became clear that he was losing passion and getting bored in his role at Learnit, the two of us sat down and planned his exit.

Even though it was difficult to think of a Learnit without Jim, we both knew it was in both parties' best interest for us to part ways. The company needed someone fresh and vibrant in the classroom, and Jim needed a new professional challenge. In sports terms, Jim had "left it all on the field" at Learnit, and I am forever grateful for that. We kept an open line of communication as he began interviewing for other positions, and I'd like to think our conversations helped give him the confidence to ask for an additional 10 percent in his salary negotiations (which he deserved and ultimately received). Unsurprisingly, Jim has done very well since, and I am incredibly proud of the part Learnit played in his professional journey.

BE PRINCIPLED

As mentioned in the last chapter, respecting people's humanity means being genuinely interested and curious about them—the fundamental gesture of respect. It also means giving them your attention, not coming down too hard on them when they make mistakes, and being both generous with and deserving of trust. It's also at the core of personal principles. Here, it starts with self-respect based on integrity and strong personal values.

INTERPERSONAL PRINCIPLES

Put simply, doing the right thing in your interactions with others means treating them with respect. For the learn-it-all leader, this is most crucial in creating an atmosphere in which your business can thrive. Employees have a great deal of stress not only on the job, but also in their personal lives, and it's good to keep that in mind. If you want them to succeed, recognize they have responsibilities outside of work and how that can impact performance. There are many ways to demonstrate your respect for others, and it starts with paying attention.

PAY ATTENTION

When you give people your full, undivided attention, you signal to them that you respect what they have to say. You might logically think that you can listen to someone while you quickly scan an email or text, but your lack of attention is more apparent than you might realize. (If you doubt this, remember the times you met with someone and they zoned out or glanced at their phones repeatedly.) You want to ensure that you show respect to the people around you by actually being present and not preoccupied. You do this by showing up on time, being attentive, and staying alert.

Be on Time

Being punctual for meetings indicates you value other people's time. It's disrespectful to stroll in late or leave early because it suggests you think your time is worth more than theirs.

Be Attentive

The best way to stay engaged and attentive during meetings and conversations is by being an active notetaker. Taking notes captures information you can refer to in the future rather than relying solely on your mental recall, and it communicates to others that what they have to share with you is important enough to write down. People will leave their interactions with you knowing that their concerns were heard and taken seriously. (Is it just me, or does it drive you nuts when waiters just nod their heads when you place an order at a restaurant without writing down a single word and return with mushrooms on your plate after you told them you hate mushrooms!)

Be Mindful of Body Language

It's not enough to just listen, you also need to be aware of your body language. It's an important and often overlooked factor in communication. If you are slumped over or yawning (which I think is the least respectful thing to do while someone is speaking to you), it appears you aren't engaged in the conversation even if you are. Instead sit upright, lean into the conversation with your shoulders square and facing your counterpart. Not only will this communicate clearly that they have your attention, it will actually improve your ability to focus.

Similarly, giving the proper amount of attention to someone else doesn't just avoid creating a negative impression, it creates a positive one. When you pay attention to someone, you make them feel special. Paying close attention to your employees' ideas shows that you value their contributions. Even if their first idea doesn't pan out, you want to encourage them to share their next one. After all, it might be a winner! Employees become more empowered and self-confident when they understand that their leader gives their ideas an appropriate amount of attention.

TURN MISTAKES INTO LESSONS

Another way you show your respect (or lack thereof) for your team members is in the way you handle their mistakes. Your employees are imperfect and will get things wrong sometimes. All too often, leaders turn their people's mistakes into personal failings or even personal attacks. This is counterproductive.

Organizations with the best cultures have high levels of psychological safety—the confidence that one can speak up without risking punishment or humiliation. A leader who separates an individual from their mistake will be able to zero in on the real issue more quickly and clearly, thereby creating a valuable learning opportunity. Many failures are caused by underlying issues and having the tools to identify root causes can prevent future problems from happening in the first place. Dan Heath's 2020 book *Upstream* is an excellent resource for learning how to address root problems and was my most recommended book of the year to friends and colleagues when it came out.

DEMONSTRATE TRUST

As a leader, you need to hold your team members accountable, but you also have to demonstrate that you trust them to work independently. When I played baseball at Arizona State, there were many practices where the coaches weren't around to ensure the players were doing what they needed to. Whether it was running drills or working in the weight room, the coaches trusted us to hold ourselves and each other accountable and to live up to the work ethic and standards Jim Brock had instilled in the Sun Devil program decades ago.

This is the kind of high-trust, high-accountability culture that you want to create as a leader. With the post-pandemic increase in demand for more flexible work schedules, companies that don't trust team members to manage their workload and deadlines without being micromanaged risk losing top talent. High performers know they can produce excellent results without management hovering over them or forcing them back into the office five days a week. As a leader of a team or an organization, it's critical you demonstrate trust in your people's ability to get the job done and give them the independence to prove you right.

But trust can be a double-edged sword. In late 2020, two of my top-tier, highly compensated employees who had been with Learnit for over twenty years approached me and asked if they could start a "side hustle." I listened to their pitch with increasing disbelief. What they were proposing was in direct competition with Learnit's core business. I gave them a couple of simple example conflict of interest scenarios and asked how they would respond.

The guys were stumped. I said, "Gentlemen, I appreciate you coming to me with your idea, and if you were starting a side business that was education-based but focused on children or anything else not in direct competition with Learnit, I'd be open to it. It's simply not acceptable for you two to start a corporate training business that would be just a rip-off of Learnit. I'm sorry, but the answer is no."

Seven months later, the pair quit and launched their own corporate training company that was a pale imitation of Learnit. They weren't even competition—competition has its own point of view. They'd simply copied just about everything from us, down to the course outlines and evaluation system I'd helped them design. The similarities were so obvious I was almost embarrassed for them and their glaring lack of originality.

We ended up having to get lawyers involved. We forced them to make some significant changes, but the betrayal stung. Learnit as an organization and I, personally, had always treated these individuals with respect and several times had gone above and beyond to accommodate their needs inside and outside of work. It was a disappointing end to a pair of twenty-year professional and personal relationships.

Despite that experience, I'd still rather actively trust people and occasionally pay the price when it's violated than walk through life suspicious and untrusting. I'm more on my guard than I once was, and I always stand my ground and take a hard line when people violate my trust, but I believe the "trust tax" is worth paying. Losing the ability to trust makes leaders overly cautious which, in turn, can cause them to miss great opportunities. Being distrustful closes you off from ideas and risk, and can lead to a poor relationship between you and the people you lead.

If you do get taken advantage of, it's important to learn from the experience and do your best to decrease the odds of it happening again. Reflect on whether there were any red flags along the way or any warning signs you might have missed. A learn-it-all will learn from even the most personal disappointments to prevent problems in the future. Instead of wasting your energy feeling victimized, focus on the learning opportunity and move forward. I genuinely believe most people have the right intentions and, in the lyrics of the Guns N' Roses song, *Bad Apples*, "Why let one bad apple spoil the whole damn bunch?"

DESERVE TRUST

An important correlation to being willing to trust others is being worthy of their trust. When you lead an organization, your people are putting their careers and their family's livelihood in your hands. They likely passed up other opportunities to join your company, and it's vital that you be worthy of that trust. Likewise, your customers are often making a big investment with your organization and need to know you can be trusted to handle it.

I've never really agreed with the sentiment that "the customer is always right," but I'm adamant that the customer's experience is at the heart of everything we do. Understanding our clients' wants and needs drives our purpose. As a leader, keeping your customer needs top of mind will help you elevate their experience and help them achieve the outcomes they want that builds long-term customer loyalty.

At Learnit, our goal has always been not only to help customers solve the challenges that they bring to us, but also to be proactive in helping them understand any they're likely to experience in the future. There are no shortcuts here. Ask your customers questions. Listen to their answers closely and thoughtfully until you understand what they need and how you can best support them. Just as with your employees, listening demonstrates respect, and you can't predict a customer's future challenges or prioritize their needs if you haven't put in this kind of respectful, human work.

If problems with a customer arise, we're committed to addressing them head-on and to doing our best to resolve them. Mistakes happen, but if we take ownership of them we can make it right even if it's on the second or third try. Customers appreciate the extra attention and willingness to deliver on promises.

Of course, sometimes customers are unreasonable and push the limits of their investment beyond what was mutually agreed to. In these cases, it's important not to shy away from conflict and push back against their demands. Doing so creates clarity and in the majority of such situations, the customer will respect you more for it and work with you to find a "win-win" resolution.

Relationships with customers should be a partnership and not a series of "my way or the highway" demands from them. If you treat a customer with respect and they don't reciprocate, you may need to make the difficult decision to fire them. Several companies are famous for having a "no assholes" policy when it comes to working with customers. Even with flagship clients, life is too short not to protect your team. Work only with customers who value your team and your partnership. If they don't, let them go. Even better, recommend they contact your competitor!

INTRAPERSONAL PRINCIPLES

Doing the right thing isn't just about the way you treat other people, it's also about your personal integrity. Having integrity and remaining consistent can be difficult. It can even be expensive, but having integrity pays off in the long run by building a solid foundation of trust between you, your employees, and your customers.

SELF-RESPECT

One thing that I've noticed from my time playing baseball and from speaking with other athletes about their experience is how valuable the early habit of self-discipline that playing sports instills becomes later in life. I recently talked with a coworker who went so far as to credit his college swim coaches for laying the foundation of his later business success. Getting up at five in the morning to get in some extra laps may have seemed miserable at the time, but it built up a solid foundation that stuck with him. I suppose some people are born with effortless self-control and discipline or have parents who gently weave it into their upbringing. The rest of us get it beaten into—I mean, have it encouraged in us by a high school or college coach.

Whether it was a parent or a coach who first insisted on discipline, learn-it-alls internalize the lesson and learn to hold themselves accountable. The ability to follow your own rules and meet the expectations you set for yourself is the foundation of self-respect (which is why it's important to make sure those expectations are reasonable).

SELF-RESPECT IS BOTH THE OUTCOME AND THE SOURCE OF SELF-DISCIPLINE.

INTEGRITY

Self-respect is also the foundation of integrity. Integrity is about knowing the right thing to do and then doing it. Every time. Even if it's painful. When you have integrity, you stand by the work you do and the commitments that you make.

Growing up with privilege, I had a lot of early exposure to people who might most accurately be described as "phony," but Walt Lembi was one of the most authentic individuals I ever met. He set the example of integrity for my siblings and me. Early on, I made the commitment to follow his example and not try to fake being who I thought people wanted me to be.

Having integrity means claiming your actions—all of them. Even the ones you may later wish to distance yourself from. If you do, there will inevitably come a time when you need to own up to something even though doing so will be unpleasant. When your integrity compels you to acknowledge missteps and shortcomings, let your self-respect demand better and put your self-discipline to work learning everything you need to know to deliver on those expectations.

OWN YOUR ENTIRE SELF—YOUR HISTORY AND YOUR FLAWS AND BE HONEST ABOUT YOUR MISTAKES. IF YOU DON'T, YOU'LL BE DOOMED TO REPEAT THEM.

You simply cannot be a great leader without integrity because the people you lead learn as much (if not more) from what you do as from what you say. If you fail yourself by over-promising and under-producing or by holding a different standard for yourself than for others, you won't inspire people to behave the way you expect. Instead they'll learn to tell you whatever you want to hear and then do whatever's easiest for them.

Exhibiting integrity, especially when it comes to owning your mistakes, creates a positive environment that permeates an organization. A leader who never acknowledges mistakes or who attempts to blame others creates a corrosive environment where employees are afraid to admit mistakes or, even worse, start to point fingers at one another. A leader's model of personal integrity is integral to an open, functioning workplace.

In 2018, Learnit switched accounting firms and as its leader, I was the one who ultimately made the decision. Unfortunately it turned out to be a disaster. The easy path would have been to pass along the blame or make excuses and dump the problem on someone else's plate. I didn't. At an all-hands meeting, I made it clear that the ill-fated decision had been mine, and that I recognized it had caused a lot of chaos for our team and customers. I apologized and shared my ideas for rectifying the situation. I then asked for their help and suggestions.

Blame-shifting erodes your integrity by creating parts of you that are internally inconsistent. External consistency is equally important, both in what you do and in how you treat others. A leader who is consistent on both levels won't, for example, make exceptions for high performers who violate the company's core values. When you allow a high performer to behave badly, it creates a toxic and demotivating environment for the rest of the team. In the long run, the negative impact on your company culture will outweigh one or two top performers.

VALUE YOUR VALUES

Every for-profit company must strive to generate a profit in order to reinvest in research and development (R&D) and to keep shareholders happy, but it's important to have integrity and to be fair, even if it occasionally means additional expenses to your bottom line. Let me give you an example. We recently hired two Customer Experience (CX) representatives within a month of each other. They had very similar skill sets and experience, but the second negotiated a salary $5,000 higher than the first. We could easily have left it at that and had a disparity in the compensation between the two. Honestly, it would have most likely worked out fine and saved us some money. But it didn't sit well with me. I reached out to the first hire and let her know we'd be bumping her salary to match the other CX rep. She, of course, was astonished and delighted. I made the decision to keep us consistent with our values, but I'm confident we earned a bit more loyalty and the trust of a new hire who knew firsthand that we're a company that treats people fairly, even before her first day on the job.

For the leaders of companies, integrity can blur the line between personal and interpersonal values. To a certain extent, the way you conduct yourself must be the way you conduct your business. Because integrity is one of my personal values, I require our sales team to do what's best for the customer the way I did what was best for the new CX hire. During discovery with a prospective client, if we determine our solutions wouldn't solve their challenges, we're honest and tell them so. Our values dictate that we don't put winning a customer's business ahead of meeting their needs, so we may even point them to a competitor who specializes in something Learnit doesn't. They appreciate our honesty and truly look at us as trusted advisers, which can lead to future referrals and future opportunities. It's clichéd, but it's true—business is a marathon, not a sprint, and doing right by your customers helps you win in the long run.

If you, as a leader, value integrity and want to see your values reflected in your company's culture, don't be afraid to make it a requirement. About ten years ago, we were having a sales contest and it came to my attention that one of our reps was falsifying his call reports. The prize was a mere one hundred dollars but, sure enough, when I confronted him with the evidence, he admitted to gaming the system. Then he tried to laugh it off.

I had to let him go. He was stunned. Fired? Him? He couldn't believe I'd actually let a top performer go over such a minor infraction. Once he got over his shock, he offered to apologize or give back his winnings, but as much as I was frustrated to lose a top performer, keeping him would have gone against my personal integrity and created a division in my team. If I'd terminate anyone else for cheating, I had to terminate him. If I'd terminate him for stealing a hundred grand, I had to terminate him for stealing a hundred dollars. Whenever it comes down to a choice between cash value and ethical ones, leave the money on the table. It's easier to earn back than your integrity.

THE RETURN ON ETHICS

As with the high-earning but dishonest sales rep I terminated and the woman we hired for more than she expected, doing the right thing can be expensive—at least in the short run. Even though downstream gains can be harder to track, I'm convinced that there's still a strong business case for doing the right thing. Beyond earning a reputation for fair dealing and the goodwill of employees and customers, I believe that more often than not, there's a real financial upside to being principled. What are the chances that a sales rep who'd cheat his teammates for a hundred bucks would walk away from an opportunity to embezzle money from the company if one ever presented itself? Obviously, there's no way to prove it, but we might have saved ourselves from much bigger losses by losing him. And the inverse is true of the CX hire. She's already added much more value to the company than the five grand I could have withheld from her.

Even if there are no direct financial rewards for treating people with respect and acting with integrity, I still think it's worth it for two completely selfish reasons: you'll feel better and you'll learn more. The root reason for both of these benefits is the same: we see the world as we are.

We all make mistakes, and I don't always live up to my own highest values, but I know that I always honestly try to do the right thing. And because I'm basically a good person, I see the world and other people as basically good. I've known enough shady characters to see the way a person's negative assessment of their own behavior slowly poisons their view of the world. Their own disappointed virtue makes them bitter. It's been my experience that people who climb to the top on the backs of others never really enjoy the view.

Secondly, people who aren't principled expect everyone else to try and cheat them. Because they're shady, they see the world as a shady place, and it makes them a lot less likely to venture out into it to explore and experiment. It's a stance that shuts down curiosity and learning. If you have a more positive personal experience of human nature, you'll see the world as a rich environment for learning. You may pay that trust tax, but the other option is to see the world as a terrible place.

CHAPTER SUMMARY

Doing the right thing requires you to behave ethically in two different domains—the interpersonal (how you treat others) and the intrapersonal (how you handle yourself). In both, respect is the cornerstone principle. Treat others with respect by giving them your full attention, by handling mistakes as opportunities for learning not occasions of shame, and by being both trusting and trustworthy. Self-respect comes from knowing you've put in the hours and the effort to earn your wins and from acting with integrity in accordance with your values.

Learn-it-all leaders work hard to protect their personal and interpersonal principles and to be curious, humble, and fully committed because they know that how they think lays the groundwork for how they perform. Having looked at this set of personal traits in the first half of the book, we'll take the next four chapters to talk about what leaders do.

PART 2

DOING

CHAPTER 5

TAKE RISKS AND MAKE DECISIONS

In the summer of 1987, I was fifteen and sitting in the dugout with my new teammates on the San Carlos All-Stars team. I was nervously waiting for practice to start when Mike Kelley, who was older than the rest of us with long black hair and a giant boombox, sat down next to me. "Hey," he said. "Have you heard this shit yet?" He punched the play button and the opening guitar riff of "Welcome to the Jungle" filled the dugout. I was blown away. It was the start of a Guns N' Roses superfandom which eventually went as far as getting a GNR logo tattoo on my shoulder when I was twenty. A decision my mother was not a fan of!

I met Axl Rose for the first time in December 2002 backstage at Madison Square Garden. He was talking with my sister, Sammy, and I got the confidence to walk up to him and say, "I'm a huge fan!"

"That's an understatement," Sammy said. "Look at this!" She pulled up my T-shirt sleeve to show Axl his band's logo tattooed on my arm.

Axl was in an uncharacteristically good mood that night. He laughed and said, "Why would you do that to yourself?"

Apparently Axl's good mood didn't last because the next day, the band announced they were scrapping the rest of the tour. I'm pretty sure it wasn't my fault.

Four years later, GNR was touring again, and I got a phone call any superfan would dream of.[14] It came from a friend of mine, Dean Delray. "Hey," Dean said, "GNR is playing the Warfield in SF this September, and Axl wants an afterparty. You think you could make that happen? A guy named Hardie from GNR's camp is going to call you, okay?"

"Absolutely!" I said. Our family owned and operated a highly-regarded boutique hotel chain in San Francisco, and Delray knew my brother and I regularly traded hotel rooms for backstage passes. It was June. September was months away. How hard could an after-party be? So when Hardie called three hours later, I was ready.

Hardie got right to the point. "Axl wants to have a party after their second show at the Warfield. Before you get all excited and say yes, you better understand it's not as simple as it seems. The band won't show up until around two in the morning, but they'll be expecting a full bar the whole time and a girl-to-guy ratio of at least 80-20. And there's no guarantee Axl will show. He just blew off Kate Moss and her crew at Bungalow 8 in New York City, so think about it first. Then give me a call in a week." And he hung up.

I immediately called my brother Taylor, and we instantly agreed

---

14   By 2006, "GNR" no longer meant the full lineup of Slash, Duff, and Izzy, but it was still Axl-freaking-Rose coming off hiatus, and everyone was excited for the tour.

that we had to make this happen, even without a clue where we would find a venue that would meet the band's requirements. We were going with Sir Richard Branson's "screw it, let's do it" decision-making philosophy of saying yes first and then figuring out how to make it work. It's a philosophy I have used several times throughout my professional career, successfully more often than not (knock on wood).

I called Hardie back and told him we were all in.

Taylor and I started calling bar and restaurant owners, confident they'd jump at a chance to throw an afterparty for Axl Rose. But we hadn't anticipated the risk involved—that of losing their liquor license by serving alcohol after-hours in violation of the law. The conversations all went something like this, "Sorry man, can't risk it, but when you find a place, let me know. I will totally be there, and I can definitely help with the invite list!"

Finally, Taylor came through with Club Whisper. It was in a seedy part of town, but the owner was pumped and said he'd handle everything we needed, including Axl's specific cigar and mixed drink requests. Now that we had a location, everything was good to go.

Or so we thought.

The night of the show, Taylor, Hardie, Club Whisper's owner, and I skipped the GNR show and met up for dinner at San Francisco's classic Original Joe's in the Tenderloin District. Taylor and I were nervous, half-joking with each other about what we'd do if no one showed up for the after-party. After all, it was a Wednesday night and the doors wouldn't open until midnight. Finally, around eleven, Taylor called the club doorman to see if anyone had shown up yet.

Taylor hung up, turned to me with a big smile on his face, and said there were about four hundred people (three-quarters women) lined up around the block in the cold weather to get in.

Relieved, we headed back to the table excited to share the good news, but the club owner pulled us aside. "Okay guys, we may have a small problem," he said. "The city might be doing some underground work in our area after hours."

"And you're just now finding this out?" I asked.

"Um, no. They sent a couple of notices, but we kind of ignored them."

"And…?" Taylor prompted.

"And there's a chance the water will be shut off from 1:00 to 8:00 a.m. this morning."

"Okay," I said, thinking it wasn't a big deal. "Let's load up on bottled water. No one will mind."

"Damon?" Taylor said. "No water, no toilets."

Good point. That would be a huge problem—four hundred party-goers with no working toilets—not good.

Thirty minutes before opening, we took a deep breath and ran through all our options. We were down to two: cancel the party and send everyone home, or go all in and hope for the best. Years after the fact, reading Annie Duke's excellent *Thinking in Bets,* I remembered our decision-making process that night because one of her key principles came into play. She recommends considering how a decision could affect your long-range happiness. We'd done a version of that, asking ourselves a younger, amped-up version of, "If the water gets cut off and the party bombs, we'll be painfully embarrassed, but a year from now, will it have significantly impacted our happiness?"

Nope.

So we rolled the dice and hoped our luck would pan out.

By 1:00 a.m., there were more than five hundred people in the club. Delray was DJing, spinning '70s and '80s rock classics, and everyone was having an incredible time. Famous rockers were turning up hoping to hang out with the elusive Axl Rose. Sebastian Bach from Skid Row was double-fisting bottles of red wine and chatting up my friends. Kirk Hammett and Robert Trujillo from Metallica were making the rounds, and so were Scott Ian from Anthrax and Whitfield Crane from Ugly Kid Joe. Even with some of the biggest rock stars from the past two decades in the mix, people were constantly stopping me saying, "Where is Axl?"

"Your guess is as good as mine," I'd answer. "But look around. Have another free drink. Go say hello to Kirk Hammett at the bar or hit up the dance floor alongside Dizzy Reed and his wife."

By a quarter to four, I'd accepted that Axl wasn't going to show up. Honestly, I didn't care. Taylor and I had pulled off the party of the year as far as I was concerned. Then, "Damon!" I felt a tug on my sleeve and turned to see my sister Chelsea. She looked stunned. "Axl's outside!"

We probably had several minutes of warning but it felt like seconds. Hardie ran over and told me to clear all my buddies out of the VIP area. We needed to make room for Axl and his entourage. Then everything changed. The energy in the room went from fun to unforgettable. Delray stopped the music midsong and queued up "Sweet Child of Mine."

The crowd parted. Axl walked in. He headed straight to the VIP section but before he sat down, he turned to the crowd. All eyes on him, he did a few seconds of his famous "snake dance." The place went nuts.

Axl sat down, was handed the cigar he'd requested, and studied it for what seemed like an eternity. Then he lit up, sat back, and seemed to thoroughly enjoy himself as a stream of women stopped by to take pictures and try to engage him in conversation. In fact, I think the only partygoer not totally delighted with how the night was going was Axl's girlfriend. She got very tired very quickly of all the female attention Axl was getting, grabbed her purse, gave him "the look," and stormed out. Axl watched her leave. Then he angrily stubbed out his cigar and followed her without saying a word to anyone.

From arrival to departure, Axl was at the party for less than half an hour, but hey—how many people can say Axl Rose showed up for their party?

Obviously, this wasn't a high-impact business decision, but I think it's a fun example of making a tough decision under pressure. Taylor and I had made a risky decision based on the information we had despite the uncertainty. In this situation we got lucky and it paid off big time! The water stayed on, Axl showed up, and Taylor and I pulled off one of the most amazing nights of our life. We also started what would be a great, fifteen-plus year friendship with Bill Hardie that led to another book's worth of great stories, from backstage with the Killers at Coachella to a private party at Bimbo's in San Francisco with the supergroup Camp Freddy for my fortieth birthday. Today Hardie's daughter Sydney is our kids' favorite babysitter!

Good business leaders make decisions and take calculated risks while understanding what the long-term implications and worst-case scenarios are if the decision doesn't generate the results they were hoping for. Luck doesn't always go your way, but when it doesn't, learn-it-all leaders learn from their failed decision and make the next one with confidence and optimism.

All leaders must make decisions and take risks, but learn-it-all leaders can never really fail because they always learn something, no matter the outcome. This gives them the courage to keep making bold decisions, taking smart risks, and learning from their own mistakes and the mistakes of others. Their courage inspires their teams, liberating them to do their best work and continue learning.

DECISION VERSUS DECISION

Decision-making is inextricably wound into leadership. In fact, McKinsey research shows that on average, executives spend almost 40 percent of their time making decisions.[15] Back in Chapter 3, I talked about the important role curiosity plays in making good decisions. In this chapter, I'll contrast the decision I made about hosting an after-party in 2006 with another I made earlier in my career that didn't turn out as well.

---

15   "Make Faster, Better Decisions," McKinsey & Company, accessed January 6, 2022, https://www.mckinsey.com/ capabilities/people-and-organizational-performance/our-insights/make-faster-better-decisions.

I stepped into the leadership role at Learnit in my late twenties just as the dot-com bubble was taking off. Everywhere I looked, my friends were becoming millionaires (at least on paper). Learnit's sales were booming right along with everything else in the Bay Area. I couldn't help thinking that leading a company was easy. We should double down and expand!

At the peak of those crazy days, I approached my dad and presented him with my ideas to increase Learnit's footprint by opening several new locations. He didn't think it was a great idea, but he heard me out and eventually agreed to open up two additional locations in San Francisco, a location in San Jose and New York, and one in the Phoenix market.

Then, before we could even open our doors at the new locations, the dot-com bubble burst and the recession came crashing down. Suddenly business wasn't easy anymore. It was terrifying. Like companies across the country, overnight, Learnit's very existence was uncertain.

My dad and I spoke often during those difficult years, and he always attempted to take some of the blame, pointing out that he'd agreed with my aggressive expansion plans. But I knew he hadn't been in favor of the decision to launch so many new locations. He'd let me, as the CEO of Learnit, make the final decision on growth initiatives for the company. The resulting dire situation Learnit was facing was the direct result of my naivete and overconfidence, and it was my responsibility to work with my team to set things right.

"Screw it, let's do it!" isn't always the right decision-making strategy, especially when a company's viability is in the balance. Had I thought about how the decision might affect the company's long-range well-being, I might have realized how much was at stake and taken a more conservative stance.

I learned a great deal from that experience and was determined to be better prepared and not make the same mistakes again. I challenged myself to learn more about decision-making, and I made sure the company built up enough cash reserves to protect it against worst-case scenarios. Risky decisions are less risky with a safety net.

Interestingly, life being what it is, I got another opportunity to make the same mistakes again six years later in the 2008 Great Recession. Fortunately, most of my leadership team from the dot-com bust was still with the company. We took a hard look at what we did well and what we could have done better in weathering that storm, and we looked for what we could learn from the experience to make better decisions this time. We pooled our knowledge and proactively addressed the downturn.

In 2002, as my team and I worked to put things back together, we focused only on what would get us through the next month. We took a piecemeal approach, addressing one issue at a time. It worked, but not well, and taught me that it's better to identify the tough decisions that need to be made early on and execute on them as soon as possible and all at once. This "rip off the Band-Aid" approach means, for example, if you need to do layoffs to get through the next twelve months, instead of periodically letting team members go, you do your best to forecast all the staffing changes you'll need to make and execute on that plan all at once. Making and acting on such tough decisions this way helps put your remaining team's mind at ease. It restores their motivation and allows them to focus on their work rather than looking over their shoulders, worrying about what changes are coming next.

Seven years later we had the (unfortunate) opportunity to enact that learning. In January 2009, in the middle of the Great Recession, we needed to downsize our staff, specifically in the sales support department. We were going to have to let someone go. It came down to a choice between a young man who had been with Learnit for two years and someone we'd hired only six months earlier. The young man—let's call him Steve—was a great guy. Everybody loved him. Walk into the sales office, and you'd find him with ESPN.com up on his laptop, talking sports. Walk into the breakroom and he'd be joking with instructors. At 4:55 p.m., Steve was out the door like it was an emergency fire drill. Courtney, the new hire, often ignored the interoffice banter, focused on her tasks, and did an excellent job. I would stop by the sales office in the early evenings on my way out and typically find our senior sales team members—Evans Hood, Matt Murawski, Sarah Finchum, and Jamie Tadlock—wrapping up their day and preparing for the next, and in the corner cubicle, Courtney was always focused and working away. I took notice of her work ethic. It wasn't so much that she was working longer hours, it was more that she took her job seriously and was dedicated to doing a stellar job.

When it came time to rip off the Band-Aid, I called in the senior sales reps who Steve supported and gave them the news—I was laying Steve off and keeping the rookie Courtney because I thought she had more to offer the company's future. I got a fair share of pushback: "Courtney isn't familiar with our accounts" or "What is the rest of the team going to say? Steve is such a nice guy and he's been around a long time." I patiently heard them out but stuck with my decision.

Fourteen years later, I can't imagine Learnit without Courtney Ritchie on the team. She has blossomed into a major leader, a member of the executive team, and my go-to person whenever I need advice or someone to keep me in check if I'm getting carried away with an idea.

Uncomfortable as our too-rapid expansion and its subsequent fallout was, I used the experience to learn lessons and prepare for the future. During the Great Recession, we adapted much more quickly. We made the tough restructuring decisions earlier and more effectively, which allowed us not only to survive our second (and objectively more severe) recession, but to thrive during it.

GET OUT OF YOUR OWN HEAD

Although my dad tried, I refused to let him take any of the blame for my overconfidence in the early 2000s. I took full ownership of my mistakes and used the pain they caused me to drive my determination to learn from them and be better prepared next time. You won't become the best leader you can be if you do anything less than take the full weight of disappointment when your decisions don't turn out as you hoped. Whether you were let down by a partner or simply had bad luck, feeling victimized or sorry for yourself will only delay your ability to learn from the experience. A leader who's afraid to own a mistake and learn from it isn't going to get anywhere. Worse, such leaders don't inspire their people. Seeing you bounce back quickly from adversity will motivate your team to do the same. A leader needs to lead, and that means taking ownership of mistakes. Portraying yourself as a victim inspires no one.

A lot of surviving and growing from a mistake comes from your mental attitude. In sports, there's a saying, "million-dollar body, ten-cent head." It refers to players with ample physical talent whose thinking gets in their way. Pure talent isn't enough to succeed at a high level in professional sports, especially if you dwell on your failures or if you blame anyone but yourself for your poor performance.

Similarly, you can have an enormous amount of business knowledge and past business victories, but if you react to failure with excuses and finger-pointing, you'll lose the opportunity to learn from your mistakes and the people who, if they'd stayed, could have provided you with insight and institutional knowledge that can help you do better next time.

LOOK FOR LEARNING

Decision-making is a skill that you develop over the years by examining your own wins and losses, observing the wins and losses of others, and studying the art and science of decision-making. Considering what a large percentage of your job decision-making is, you need to get it right. (Send me a message on LinkedIn or email, and I'll happily inundate you with great decision-making resources.)

One thing I learned in my deliberate study of decision-making is that people often narrow a decision down to two options and then try to pick between them. If you tend to get stuck in an either-or mindset, it's good to take a step back and try to add additional options you haven't considered yet. For example, let's say you are looking to hire an executive assistant. You might ask yourself, "Should I try to recruit and hire someone from outside our organization or promote someone from within?" This makes the decision a binary choice.

When you search for a third option—perhaps considering an outsourced firm that specializes in virtual assistants—you begin to increase your chance of a great outcome. According to *Decisive*, by the Heath brothers, what they call "narrow framing" causes you to focus on the immediate choice to the extent that you miss other options. Just the act of searching for alternatives improves your understanding of the situation. Even if you do end up picking one of your original two options, it's more likely to be the correct choice having considered a third or fourth possibility.

In the same way that additional options can lead to better decisions, so can additional inputs. When you've spent a lot of time going over the ins and outs of a specific decision, you can become hung up on the details and miss the big picture. Instead, recognize that your vantage point may not give you the best view of the situation. I often ask members of my team for their opinions on upcoming decisions. This doesn't mean that I will necessarily act on their advice, but simply seeking out different points of view helps ensure better outcomes.

Although it's good to have more options and to receive more input, there is a limit. You don't want to get input from, say, thirty people. Too much information can confuse the issue. Have a few trusted people that you can turn to for advice in certain situations. And always make it clear that the final decision—and the accountability—rests with you. Your team should understand this and be willing to get behind you no matter which direction you take.

Approaching decisions in a methodical manner will help clarify issues and identify holes in your thinking. I like to use a decision journal.[16] It's a notebook dedicated to important decisions in which I record the reasoning behind the need to make a decision and list different options and potential results—including worst-case scenarios. I've found it to be a useful tool on two levels: it helps me make complex decisions and it provides a record of my predictions

---

16   For a great article on keeping a decision journal, see https://fs.blog/decision-journal/.

and process. I periodically review it to learn from the decisions I've made, see how accurately (or terribly) my projects matched reality, and identify blind spots I didn't see at the time.

KEEP TAKING RISKS

Inevitably, some risks you take won't pay off, but shying away from taking them can cause your organization to miss out on big opportunities. I took a risk when I decided to look for talent at the height of uncertainty during the pandemic. That risk paid off, but even had Learnit not acquired the outstanding people we did, it would have been worth taking the shot. It wasn't a decision that could have bankrupted the company and the possible rewards easily outweighed the worst-case scenario. Taking these kinds of smart risks can give you a significant advantage.

A lot of people think that you need to be fearless to take big risks and succeed, but that isn't the case. I still have to confront fear when I make big decisions, but I've learned to face it and to remind myself that making too-cautious decisions can be as risky as making risky ones. The failures of timidity are less obvious and don't so obviously attach to the nondecision maker, but they're just as bad for your company. And, in the immortal words of Geddy Lee, "When you choose not to decide, you still have made a choice." (And although I'm not a superfan of the band Rush the way I am of Guns N' Roses, I think I'm better guided by his lyrics than by Axl's "You can have anything you want/But you better not take it from me.")

CHAPTER SUMMARY

The "screw it, let's do it!" approach to decision-making is a viable option for decisions when possible bad outcomes are recoverable.

For higher-stakes decisions, other frameworks and tools (like decision journals) are useful in guiding you to better decisions. You must dig deep and make time to think and process how you make decisions. Learn-it-all leaders understand decision-making is a critical skill and invest time and effort in honing theirs.

There's always an element of risk in making a decision, but even though it's entirely the leader's to take, learn-it-all leaders give the credit to and share the rewards with their team.

CHAPTER 6

BUILD GREAT TEAMS

Reading Herb Kelleher's autobiography *Nuts!: Southwest Airlines' Crazy Recipe for Business and Personal Success* several years ago, one story caught my attention and has stayed with me ever since. Kelleher calls the anecdote the "Ten Minute Turn." At the time, Southwest was fighting for its survival, embroiled in a David-and-Goliath battle against major airlines. Southwest was running out of options and nearing bankruptcy.

The executive team, led by Bill Franklin, did some quick math and realized their only option was to empty the garbage, clean the planes, and refuel them in only ten minutes. Industry veterans assured him it couldn't be done. Everyone who knew anything knew it was impossible. So Kelleher and his team recruited and hired people who didn't know anything about the airline industry. He made it a priority to avoid anyone with a "that's not the way things work" mindset. Instead he looked for people with what he calls a "we can and we will" attitude. I call them learn-it-alls.

Learn-it-all leaders hire a diverse team of coachable learn-it-alls from whom they, themselves, can learn. They find great people, figure out their strengths and focus on them. They then build a culture of curiosity and learning where everyone is set up to win.

HIRE UNITED DIFFERENCES

In Chapter 3, I touched on the value of seeking input from a team diverse enough to spot and contribute a wide range of possibilities. I want a workforce diverse in age, gender, ethnicity, and work experience because such diversity leads to a wide range of perspectives. A team in lockstep agreement on every issue will have blind spots that can be detrimental while a broad range of viewpoints increases a leader's options and decision-making ability.

HIRE FOR DIVERSITY OF OPINION AND COMMONALITY OF PRINCIPLES.

Learnit has developed and iterated on our core values over the years. We take them seriously and do our best to live them out, not just have them hidden on the website. When we evaluate a potential new hire, our decision to hire or not is based in large part on whether the individuals demonstrate our core values. These, in an easy-to-remember acronym, are:

- **L**-Lifelong learning
- **E**-Embrace Change
- **A**-Act Like Owners
- **R**-Rally around the Customers
- **N**-Nurture a Growth Mindset

In short, we want learn-it-alls who are committed, humble, curious, principled, and brave. (And if that sounds familiar, see Chapters 1 through 5.)

It can be risky to prioritize values over experience to the extent that we do, but I believe it pays off. If you want to build an effective team, you need to find people who exhibit all the qualities that you value in your organization: humility, curiosity, and work ethic. It's almost impossible to take an experienced person who doesn't have the attributes you're looking for and change them. It's much easier to take someone who already has those attributes and find a position where they can excel. Joe Patti is a perfect example.

Joe came to us on the recommendation of his cousin, Heather D'Angelo. Heather is a classic example of the kind of learn-it-all team member we look for. She exemplified our values and was also super sharp and hard-working. She moved on to a ride-share company after her tenure at Learnit, but like many of our alumni, when she runs into talented people she thinks would be a good fit, she sends them our way.

Joe was in the process of moving west from New Jersey and needed a job. Heather told him Learnit was a great place to work and then gave me a call to say she thought I would love Joe's attitude and energy. We quickly set up a meeting and when Joe came in, I could see that he would be a great fit for our culture. He shared our values and was motivated, energetic, and friendly. Plus he had Heather's recommendation. He didn't have a lot of previous business experience, but I thought that with his "go-getter" attitude, Joe would be a great fit for sales.

Right away, he proved himself to be a true learn-it-all. He took every class I recommended and read all the books I suggested. I thought he'd be one of our top salespeople in no time. I was wrong. As the months wore on, it became clear to me that Joe wasn't happy. He wasn't doing as well as he or I had expected, but it wasn't from a lack of effort. I invited him out to dinner to find out what was going on. Over a beer, Joe admitted that he wasn't grasping the sales stuff and told me that things just weren't working out for him. He was discouraged and half-ready to admit defeat. I think a lot of managers would have just agreed with him, let him go, and wished him luck. But I knew that if we could just find the right spot for him, Joe could flourish at Learnit.

I told him that I saw how much effort he was putting in and that I appreciated it. He was worried that he was wasting our time, but I reassured him. I knew he had a love for technology and being the center of attention, so I suggested that he apply to be an instructor. I told him I would pair him with a mentor and we'd see if that role would be a better match for his strengths and abilities. Joe seemed encouraged and approached being an instructor with all the motivation that he had put into sales. But this time, in the right position, he succeeded, eventually becoming one of our most requested and best instructors. I saw the learn-it-all attributes of commitment, humility, and curiosity in Joe and believed he could learn the rest once we got him into the right job.

HIRE TOP TALENT

Once I left my Batman days behind, I've never claimed to have any so-called "superpowers." But if I were pressed on the question and had to pick one, I'd say it's my ability to attract smart, passionate people and align their strengths with our company's needs using what I've dubbed the 3F Formula: find great people, figure out their strengths, and focus on those strengths.

Find great people. Identifying great people for your company is key. At Learnit, we've developed a strong culture and have been able to attract new hires aligned with it, the majority from internal referrals. When evaluating a candidate, I believe it's important to focus less on experience and accolades and more on curiosity and untapped ability.

According to a 2020 LinkedIn study, "eighty-two percent of employees rated employee referrals above all other sourcing options to yield the best return on investment (ROI)."[17]

Curiosity isn't always easy to identify in the interview process. We typically structure specific questions for candidates related to professional growth around hobbies they enjoy, the last book they read, or we ask for an example of a skill they have recently learned. If a candidate is stumped by these questions and can't think of a book they've read in the last year or come up with a skill they've recently taken an interest in learning, it's a genuine concern for us. It most likely means the candidate lacks a growth mindset and wouldn't thrive in a culture of passionate lifelong learners.

Figure out their strengths. Once you have great people on board, it is your responsibility as a leader to figure out their strengths and leverage them. I learned this principle having been fortunate enough to have played for three of the greatest college baseball coaches in recent history (Andy Lopez, John Noce, and Jim Brock). Great coaches identify where each player will have the most impact and

---

17   Mike Stafiej, "Employee Referral Statistics You Need to Know for 2020 (Infographic)," LinkedIn, January 13, 2020, https://www.linkedin.com/pulse/employee-referral-statistics-you-need-know-2020-mike-stafiej/.

deploy them accordingly. Sure, one guy might be able to play third base, but he still might do better as a pitcher.

Leaders should be willing to spend a little extra time to find the right spot for an employee who has the obvious potential to be a great fit for your organization. You've already seen two examples of this principle in the story I just told about Joe and in the one about Carly Lutz from Chapter 3 who was smart and ambitious enough for us to hire as a salesperson. She had the skills to do well there, but it wasn't until she created and moved into the role of community and events strategist that she became an enormous asset to Learnit.

Focus on their strengths. In the long-standing debate of "Should you work on improving weaknesses or elevating strengths?," I am a big believer in the latter. Sure, it helps to improve weaknesses, but I find helping individuals develop their strengths dramatically accelerates their growth. It's also critical to align people's interests with at least some of their assigned responsibilities. Someone may be very good at something but really hate it. Finding the magic formula for passions and strengths is key!

Some managers may hesitate to hire high-caliber talent in the mistaken belief that these new hires might outshine them. This is entirely the wrong attitude. A great leader wants to bring on the absolute best minds available, and not only for the organization's benefit. Learn-it-all leaders thrive when we surround ourselves with the best. You don't want people who will make you *look* better, you want people who will make you *be* better. A-players hire A-players.

There's also a common worry that top-level talent will simply outgrow your organization, and it may. It's happened many times at Learnit. But I have absolutely no regrets. When truly excellent people join your team, even for a short amount of time, they bring with them an immense opportunity for you to learn from them and to push yourself as a leader. If you recruit the best people, some of them are going to move on, it's true. But this simply grows your network of talented alumni, which can pay off in unforeseen ways.

HIRE COACHABLE PLAYERS

Confidence is great, but when we're hiring, I'm more impressed with people who are willing to take advantage of offers of help than I am with people who say, "I've been doing this for years, I know what I am doing and have it all figured out." If a prospective hire is so confident that they have closed themselves off to new learning opportunities, it's a red flag for me. With the pace of change in today's world, organizations need teams with the ability to adapt and beginners' minds that are open to collaboration. We look for people who are willing to work together and who see collaborations as learning opportunities.

Hiring this kind of coachable employee is essential to our long-term success. During the onboarding process, we assign certain books and classes and then watch to see if the new hires demonstrate our core value of lifelong learning. Are they engaged in it or just going through the motions? Even during the interview phase, when we check someone's references, it's common for us to ask questions about whether or not the prospective employee is open to new ideas. It's all about finding that coachable mindset that can grow along with the organization instead of someone who is set in their ways and closed off to change and improvement.

A good leader looks for people who are energized by learning opportunities and new ideas. Over-the-top energy isn't necessary, but you do want employees who are excited about their work and want to challenge themselves, not stick with the status quo all the time. If employees aren't interested in ways they can develop themselves, they aren't going to be looking for ways to better their team and our organization. Worse, their lack of passion will be picked up by the people that they lead, their peers, and in certain situations, customers as well.

I learned the value of hiring for coachability explicitly a few years ago when we recruited a sales executive from a competitor. I welcomed him to Learnit, gave him a couple of books, and asked him to block out forty-five minutes of each workday to read them.[18] I let him know I'd be re-reading the books with him and that we'd meet bi-weekly to discuss his top takeaways and how he could leverage his learnings in his new role.

Over the next few weeks, the guy found every excuse in the proverbial book to avoid meeting to talk about the actual ones I'd given him. When we finally sat down together, it was immediately clear to me just by glancing at the book that he hadn't even opened it. I couldn't believe it! He'd been in sales for over a decade so I suppose he thought, "What could a book possibly teach me?" He wasn't curious about learning new techniques or interested in upskilling himself for our ever-changing work landscape. Sure, he had some past customer relationships that could have boosted his sales, but he wasn't open to coaching. We let him go after only ninety days when we determined he wasn't, as Jim Collins would say, "the right person on the bus." I'll take someone with little experience and few

---

18   It's critically important for you as a leader to create space in the workday for your team members' professional development. Expecting them to do it on their own time is a recipe for failure. At Learnit, we call it giving team members LTO (learning time off).

contacts who is coachable and hungry to learn it all over a know-it-all twenty-year sales veteran any day!

As a leader, you're in a great position to model this trait for your teams. I take advantage of as many learning opportunities as possible—from executive coaching to Learnit leadership courses—and I still ask for and act on the advice I get from mentors. I also try to model coachability by being open to feedback (positive or negative) from anyone and at every level of my organization.

CREATE A TEAM CULTURE

Once you've assembled a diverse team of talented, coachable people, they deserve a great culture in which to thrive. This is your job but it's not something you can create the way you build out a new office. You can't create culture directly. It's an outgrowth of your lived (not merely posted) values. If your company is rooted in strong, positive values which are woven into your conversations and presentations and reinforced in your vision and decisions, these values will permeate your organization from top to bottom. And this will form its culture.

In creating a learn-it-all culture, it's vital that you lead by example. If you're not a learn-it-all, how can you be excited about what you're trying to accomplish? If you don't want to invest time in your own professional growth, how are you going to lead a team or build trust with customers that you have the insights and know how to guide them toward their desired outcomes? If you're not continuously looking to evolve, learn new skills, and take chances, you won't reach your full potential. When your team sees you're dedicating time to staying abreast of current events and researching trends in industries (or even for specific customers), they will follow your direction.

I highly recommend allowing your team members to explore the books, magazines, and journals they prefer to gain insights for themselves. The company should support them by allowing them to expense any related monthly or annual fees. Several of our team members have subscriptions to the *Wall Street Journal, Harvard Business Review,* and local business journals.

I want everyone on our team to be interested in improving their business acumen, aware of the current business climate, and thinking about how Learnit can have a positive impact and support our customers with their upskilling and reskilling goals.

As an example, we model our value of lifelong learning by regularly setting aside time in team meetings explicitly for learning. We ask each team member to come prepared with two insights from the past week that could impact Learnit or our customers. We then brainstorm ways to put those insights into action.

CURATE YOUR CULTURE

Of course, it would be great if employees never had problems with leadership or with each other, but that's not a realistic expectation— your people are *people*, after all. And if they're passionate people who care about what your company does and how it gets done, differences of opinion are bound to come up. When they do, frame them to yourself and your team as the opportunities they are for learning and for strengthening your company culture by living out your values.

I've found that learning from interpersonal conflict or concerns is essential to creating and maintaining a culture of learn-it-alls. It's a very visible way Learnit demonstrates the value we place on improvement and growth, but it's also generalizable to other companies. How you handle conflict has an enormous impact on the health of your culture and the strength of your team, and it plays out primarily in three different ways: how open you are to other people's ideas, how you handle other people's problems, and how you respond to negative feedback.

NEW IDEAS

Soliciting ideas and seeking input from the people you lead not only helps you improve, it makes them more likely to share potentially impactful insights with you. The expectation shouldn't be that every idea they share with you will automatically be implemented, but you want your people to know that you are listening and that their input is important to you.

This lesson applies to every level of your organization. It may be obvious that good ideas can come from your trusted senior team but don't forget MBWA (Management By Walking Around). Everyone from the administrative support team to your engineering folks will very likely have thoughts and opinions that could contribute to a better team and organization and you should proactively seek them out.

Knowing they aren't just individual contributors with assigned tasks but can have a real impact on their team and perhaps the overall organization is hugely motivating. People get more invested in companies and initiatives they feel they have a hand in creating. Just knowing they are being heard will motivate them and, when one of their ideas is acted on and they are given the credit and recognition they deserve, it supercharges that team member and others, making them more likely to generate even more and better ideas.[19] It builds a virtuous cycle of engagement, teamwork, and contribution which is critical to building an engaged and curious culture.

Matt Murawski, a senior executive on our leadership team, comes to mind as an example of someone who thinks outside the box and brings exciting ideas to the table. Matt joined Learnit as a salesperson in 1999 and has grown with us. He has played a critical role in everything from leading the sales team to developing and launching Learnit's partner channel.

It would be hard to imagine where Learnit would be today if we hadn't taken advantage of Matt's innovative mind. From coming up with customized solutions for his customer base to creating a company-wide subscription model, he's transformed the way we serve our customers to better meet their needs.

CHALLENGES

If you create a culture where employees know that you trust them enough to try to solve challenges on their own but that your door is always open if they need your help, it builds their confidence and autonomy. If you're the type of leader who gets frustrated, lacks patience, or becomes defensive when people raise concerns, you'll motivate your employees to keep problems from you. Part of creating a strong team is ensuring that team members know that you will be open to providing guidance when necessary to resolve problems

---

19   One of the worst, most culture-killing traits of poor leaders is to take credit for someone else's ideas or wins. I have seen it happen, and it kills your team's motivation. People will resent the leader and the idea mill will dry up instantly. You can't do all the work or generate all the ideas or innovations yourself. Tap into your talented team eager to supply you with innovative ideas!

rather than distributing blame. This benefits both your customers and your bottom line.

Only once the problems are addressed will the big wins start to arrive. And when they do, it's important to recognize and celebrate them. You don't need to do anything too elaborate, but people just want to know that their efforts are noticed and appreciated. A recent Gallup study shows one of the key contributors to low employee engagement and turnover is a lack of recognition or praise within the organization.[20] As Bill Walsh, the legendary coach of the San Francisco 49ers said, "Few things offer a greater return on less investment than praise—offering credit to someone in our organization who has stepped up and done the job." Publicly praising people for living your company's values also pays triple dividends. It rewards excellence in the top performer, inspires everyone else to the same, and affirms the values that create your culture.

NEGATIVE FEEDBACK

As you ask employees for their honest feedback, you have to prepare yourself to hear things that you may not like. If you communicate to your team that you have an open door and welcome their ideas and constructive feedback, and if you ask them to take ownership of their mistakes, you need to do your part and not get defensive or upset and place blame. If you are perceived as defensive or get frustrated with mistakes easily, they will withhold information or hide mistakes just like—as those of us who have kids know—children will. Instead of creating an opportunity to improve your organization or a learning opportunity for that individual, you are at risk of creating a secretive and siloed culture where people cover up mistakes and

20   Jim Harter, "U.S. Employee Engagement Slump Continues," Gallup, April 25, 2022, https://www.gallup.com/workplace/391922/employee-engagement-slump-continues.aspx.

even point fingers. It's difficult to lead a great team of top talent if your culture lacks psychological safety, and you will miss out on great learning opportunities.

When the pandemic first started and there was a lot of chaos and uncertainty, I established daily virtual meetings at Learnit. I wanted to check in with people and reassure them in a time of crisis. I figured if I were going to err, I'd err on the side of over-communication. Even though the team was spread out and distanced, I knew it was important to our culture that they still feel connected so that the pandemic wouldn't negatively affect the way we worked together more than it absolutely had to.

Of course, intense communication can make some employees feel like they aren't trusted or valued, and it wasn't long before our COO, who was relatively new at the time, let me know he felt like he was being micromanaged. The first response that came to mind for me was to be defensive and explain that he wasn't being micromanaged at all! But that would have only undermined the growth mindset and coachability culture I'm striving to create at Learnit.

I didn't think I was managing him too closely but over the years, I've learned that a little humility can go a long way. In the end, we talked through the issue and there were no hurt feelings or frustrations. Looking back, I'm proud that I created a culture at Learnit where a relatively new hire felt comfortable enough to come to me and provide me with constructive feedback.

INVEST IN YOUR PEOPLE

Taking the time to build a learn-it-all culture attracts a higher-caliber team. Smart, talented people can work anywhere, but they want to work somewhere where they believe in the purpose and vision of the company and where they will be able to develop professionally. This is increasingly true of the younger people who join the workforce. And tomorrow's leaders are demanding it. Many companies are finding that investing in the education and growth of their people is a more effective and compelling form of employee retention than additional vacation days or bonuses. At Learnit, we benefit from both sides of this positive trend in the people and organizations we attract as workers and as clients.

Seventy-six percent of employees in a recent survey said they are more likely to stay with an organization that offers continuous training opportunities.[21]

Of the many different outcomes we try to help organizations with, the one that's showing the most aggressive growth is the ability to recruit, hire, and retain great talent by providing a culture rich in learning opportunities to advance employee career growth and internal mobility. In fact, helping companies promote from within is our single largest demand area. These companies have smart, capable people with a great deal of institutional knowledge who have never had the opportunity to manage people before. Once they would have needed to move to a new company to get a significant increase in pay and title. Increasingly, companies are recognizing the value of retention and of investing in professional development for team members at all levels of the organization. It's an exciting time to be a learn-it-all leader and to see the impact learning has and will have on the workforce.

---

21   Ana Casic et al., "The State of L&D in 2022," TalentLMS, accessed January 6, 2023, https://www.talentlms.com/employee-learning-and-development-stats.

CHAPTER SUMMARY

Without a doubt, my favorite thing about Learnit's twenty-seven-plus-year history has been the people who have walked through our doors and joined the team. I have had the incredible fortune of being able to surround myself with talented individuals, and it's been a true privilege to see their careers blossom here at our organization and in their subsequent endeavors.

It takes time and effort to find the right people, but if you are laser-focused on finding untapped talent and people with strong values, you set yourself up for long-term success. Learn-it-all leaders hire a humble, curious team and set every member up to win by creating a culture that's welcoming, warm, forgiving, and focused on individuals' strengths. They build great teams of top performers who put a premium on learning.

And winning.

CHAPTER 7

PLAY TO WIN

When I was recruited by Pepperdine to play for Coach Lopez, he was clear about his goal. He set his sights on the College World Series. At the time, no one thought that Pepperdine could compete at that level against college baseball powerhouses like LSU (Louisiana State University) and the University of Miami.

Coach Lopez 100 percent believed we could.

I'll never forget the time at practice when one of our star pitchers wore a University of Miami shirt. Coach Lopez said, "Take that damn shirt off right now! Don't put that team on a pedestal!" At the time, Miami was one of the top teams in the country, and he didn't want us idolizing them or any of the other top programs for one minute. He taught us to believe in our own ability, to focus on what we could control, and that if we did, we could compete and beat anyone!

Coach Lopez's attitude taught me that great leaders think *big*. They aren't satisfied with the status quo (in this case winning our league).

They always have some ultimate, larger goal in mind. It's a vision of a future that's bigger than present reality suggests is possible.

Developing a vision can start with a simple list of goals, but it shouldn't end there. Leaders with vision look for areas where they can stretch those goals, and they strive for the moon shot, a level of achievement that ordinary leaders dismiss as impossible. Leaders with that kind of outsized vision inspire their teams and instill confidence in their players. I married a woman with this type of vision. She's strong, fiercely loyal, and beyond passionate about things she believes in. Luckily for me, she's my biggest champion, which gives me the confidence I need to lead Learnit.[22]

> ### BUSINESS, LIKE SPORTS, IS COMPETITIVE— GREAT LEADERS PLAY TO WIN, AND WINNING STARTS WITH VISION.

BIG WINS

It may seem like a small detail that one of our pitchers was wearing the logo of another team, but to Coach Lopez, it was a sign that we didn't see ourselves playing on Miami's level. For his vision to be realized, he knew he had to start by changing our mindset. After all, Pepperdine was the underdog in the fight, a David to Miami's Goliath. We couldn't afford to accept we were inferior in any way.

I spoke to Coach Lopez for the first time in thirty years in September of 2022 and asked him what it was like for him to win the world

---

22   Together, we make a good team and have been blessed to build a beautiful family. Some say iron sharpens iron and this is true of our relationship. She never stops encouraging me or inspiring me to become the best version of myself. I strive to do the same for her and our children in return.

series back in 1992. He said, "Damon, I have a great story for you! The night before the series began, we attended a banquet with all the other teams. All the bigtime programs and coaches were there—Miami with their head coach Ron Fraser, Texas with Cliff Gustafson, Cal State Fullerton's Augie Garrido—it was literally the *Who's Who* of college baseball programs and legendary coaches and me, Andy Lopez, an unknown thirty-nine-year-old out of Los Angeles.

"The MC introduced each team and had the coach come up and say a few words. Finally, it was our turn. The host announced us. 'Now I would like to call up *Eddie* Lopez from Pepper*dime* University, our Cinderella-story team out of Malibu, California. Let's welcome Coach *Lopez* up to say a few words.'

"I kept my composure," Coach Lopez told me. "But when we got out to the team bus, I asked the driver to step outside for a few minutes while I talked to my team. Once he left, I turned to the guys and told them, 'Gentlemen, it doesn't bother me that the MC called me *Eddie* Lopez and mispronounced our school name. I can live with that. No one expected us to get here. Gentlemen, we have two options. One—we get our ass kicked over the next two days, which everyone expects to happen, and head home with our tails between our legs. Two—we get out on the field, play the way we know we are capable of, prove we belong here, and kick these other teams' f**king asses!'

"Damon, as you know, the rest is history."

When Learnit was starting out, we were in a similar position—unknown and outmatched. The industry leader at the time was Catapult Inc., owned and operated by IBM. It was easy for any company looking for computer training to just go with the status quo and contract with them, knowing that if it didn't work out, no one would fault their decision. It was risky for decision-makers to invest their L&D budget with an unknown entity like Learnit. We had to fight to show we belonged. We had to be better than the competition, and not just a little bit better. We had to come up with ways to differentiate ourselves and better serve our customers' training needs.

Learnit accomplished this by developing a unique approach to computer training. In the '90s, in-person computer training classes were typically one to three days long. We took the opposite approach and structured the content of our courses into ninety-minute, bite-size learning modules which allowed for flexibility in scheduling, increased retention, and delivered more focused learning. By disrupting the computer training market, we found a way to win. The industry leaders thought we were crazy and that short, modular training would never work. Twenty-seven-plus years later, everything is about microlearning these days. Walt Lembi and his big moon shot vision were ahead of his time, but his innovative approach won us a seat at the table, and we never looked back.

TEAM WINS

As a leader, you'll struggle to get your team members to reach their potential if you don't provide them with the vision and purpose that makes all their effort worthwhile. Leaders must inspire their teams and celebrate even small victories. Be clear that playing to win means winning as a team. Obviously, this means not taking credit for the work of others, but it also means celebrating people when their ideas or efforts have a positive impact. If you are genuinely happy when members of your team succeed, they will notice and continue to work hard for you. Creating a culture of "team first" is imperative for long-term profitability and creates a flywheel effect for acquiring and retaining top talent.

WIN WITH INTEGRITY

Some people interpret "playing to win" as doing whatever it takes to win at any cost. I'm very competitive and love to win, but it's important to do so without violating my principles. My team knows that I am okay with mistakes but won't tolerate deliberate breaches of our values. We never deceive customers into believing we can deliver on promises we can't in order to win a deal. Team members who do alienate the customer and set other team members up to fail. Doing right by your customers and putting teammates in a position to win makes you a great and valuable team player.

Because I hire learn-it-alls, I have a team of people who are committed, humble, curious, and principled, and I don't need to do much policing or policy-making. I tell them we play to win, but we play by our core values. We put our best effort forward and in doing so, have the confidence we need to win.

Still, we don't win every time.

WINS FROM LOSSES

Early in my career, I took it hard when we didn't win in a competitive situation. Whether it was a large sales opportunity or losing a great team member to a competitor, I got frustrated, took it personally, and let it linger, negatively affecting me and my team. As the years went on, I realized you can't win every time (but you can always prepare and put forth your best effort). I was able to learn from the losses and move on. I call that a win.

I recently read Ryan Holiday's *The Ego is the Enemy*, which helped me further reframe taking losses personally. Holiday points out what an enormous waste of energy it is to be overly concerned with your own dignity. You need to realize that nothing you do will end up exactly the way you wanted it to. You have to roll with the punches and be able to pivot. Taking yourself too seriously can cause you to be too cautious and prevent you from achieving the big wins because you aren't sticking your neck out there enough. Another great book I highly recommend for those of us who struggle to deal with losing in the business world or who fear being turned down is *Go for No! Yes is the Destination, No is How You Get There* by Andrea Waltz and Richard Fenton. It's a great book that helps you understand the importance of getting out of your comfort zone.

EVERYBODY WINS?

I think one reason some people in the business world abandon their integrity is that to them, winning is a zero-sum game. They believe, wrongly, that if one company or one person wins, everyone else loses. I've never believed this to be true in business, even if it is the way baseball works. As I've said before, I'm fine when one of my team members moves on from Learnit to another career opportunity they believe is better for themselves and their families. Yes, we're losing a valued team member, but we're also gaining a loyal alumnus contact at a potential customer, one who appreciates the time spent with us.

Try to make certain that's the case. Burning bridges with an employee who has worked hard for you and has made the decision to leave will not only harm your culture (the ex-employee will talk to your current team and share with them your immature approach to their departure), it is also shortsighted. You always want to keep the door open for a great employee who left. You never know; sometimes the grass isn't greener on the other side, and they'll want to come back.

Even when it comes to competing against other firms, zero-sum thinking is shortsighted. When we partner with competitors or partners, we always make sure we deal fairly with them. Learnit has had its share of clients stolen by untrustworthy partners, but I don't believe they ended up the winner in the long run. They were "penny-smart and pound-foolish." If you gain the reputation of being an untrustworthy partner, it will hurt you with prospective clients and partners, and your employees will likely emulate your win-at-all-costs mindset. This creates a toxic environment where no one trusts anyone and communication breaks down.

One of the frustrations when you end up losing a deal is the feeling that you've been left with nothing to show for all your efforts, but that's never the case for a learn-it-all leader. For us, failure is always an opportunity to learn. If you've recently lost a bid, I highly recommend reaching out to the prospect and asking them why they selected the other vendor. If you approach them in a nondefensive way and communicate that you are okay with their decision and just want to learn what you could have done differently or better, you will be surprised by how open the prospect will be with you. It's an invaluable learning opportunity for you and your team. Sure, it can be humbling or even frustrating, but it gives you something to build on.

Even if feedback from the lost client isn't available, it's still often helpful to dive right into a postmortem after a loss. What could you have done differently? Where can you improve? When you analyze the details, you'll often find something that you overlooked or could have done differently. Understanding your shortcomings only increases your chances to win in the future. By focusing on improvement, learn-it-all leaders are more likely to adapt and improve their performance at the next opportunity, which could be a big win waiting to happen!

Playing to win is always about the future. There's no way to win a game that's already over, and no way to win a deal that you missed out on. If you're always looking backward, obsessing over failures or worried about how you look to others, then you don't have the focus on the future that's necessary to go for the big win. To quote legendary 49ers coach Bill Walsh one more time, "Winners act like winners before they're winners…The culture precedes positive results. It doesn't get tacked on as an afterthought on your way to the victory stand. Champions behave like champions before they're champions: they have a winning standard of performance before they're winners."

CHAPTER SUMMARY

The learn-it-all leader knows that business isn't necessarily a zero-sum game and holds a clear and inspiring vision of what winning big looks like. They then prepare, give their best effort, and compete, knowing they have the opportunity to learn something along the way regardless of the final score.

But you can't win with a losing team, so learn-it-all leaders invest in coaching their players.

CHAPTER 8

COACH YOUR TEAM

One morning in 2000, my dad and I were standing in the lobby of Learnit's 45 Montgomery Street location talking with Britt Miller, the leader of our sales team. My dad loved Britt's passion, intensity, and work ethic, and he loved giving him a hard time, but that morning, I could see he was losing interest in the conversation. His focus had drifted to the woman working at the reception desk. She was working from a list of past customers, calling and upselling them on future classes. "Hey Britt," my dad said, "that young lady at the front desk has made more outbound calls in the past thirty minutes than I bet your sales team probably has made all month! You should promote her to the sales team!"

The woman who'd impressed my dad was Dalit Lewis, who had started at Learnit as an IT intern six months prior. Dalit had come to the US from Israel where she'd served as a tank sergeant in the Israel Defense Forces. She was disciplined and competitive with a phenomenal work ethic. And an equally strong accent. When Britt and I took my dad's advice and offered her a chance in sales, she thought we were joking. We weren't. "But my accent?" she said. "English is my second language, I don't think customers will understand me." We assured her that with her discipline and hard work combined with the right support from her sales manager (Britt), we believed she would do great things.

Several months later, I asked Dalit to join my grandfather and me for our weekly tradition of breakfast at iconic Sears Fine Food in downtown San Francisco. My grandfather, a WWII veteran, took a liking to her right away when I introduced her as "the tank sergeant."

"Knock on doors, tank sergeant! Don't be afraid to make those cold calls! That's what it takes to win in sales!" he told her.

Dalit went on to generate more than $30 million in sales for Learnit over her amazing career, working in a field that she would never have considered had my dad not suggested it. Had we not been willing to invest the time, energy, and patience in coaching Dalit's raw talent, Learnit wouldn't have reaped the rewards of her awesome approach to sales.

But Dalit deserves 100 percent of the credit. Her willingness to learn, work ethic, and positive attitude made her a leader in her field, and I'm sure she will pass those strengths down to her three wonderful daughters. She certainly made a strong impression on my grandfather. Even when he was over a hundred years old, when we got together, he always asked me, "How is Learnit? Is the tank sergeant still knocking on doors?"

A coach watches their players closely, offers insights and perspective, and invests effort in developing talent. They don't micromanage or attempt to take control of every situation.

DON'T BE A HERO

In my opinion, the best sales management book of all time is Mike Weinberg's *Sales Management. Simplified.* From it (and from having had Mike work with me and my team directly for years), I learned the important difference between being a hero and a hero-maker. The leader who jumps in and takes over is taking the "hero" approach. Mike gives the example of a sales leader who jumps in on a sales call and takes over control of the conversation with the customer, which doesn't teach the sales executive anything. In sales management (or any management role), a leader's goal should be to help coach your employees to learn, not to jump in and do the work for them. This can take quite a lot of self-restraint, and I admit that I haven't always been able to resist the temptation of getting involved, but I've found that those (sometimes difficult) investments of time and patience pay off.

A favorite example that I share with sales leaders dates back to November 2005. At the time, Learnit had recently onboarded Evans Hood as a new member of our sales team. I decided to join Evans on her first in-person sales meeting with a public accounting firm. On our drive out to Redwood City, we went through my typical checklist of discovery meeting questions: "Who are we meeting with and what are their roles? Why have they agreed to meet with us? What outcomes would we like to achieve?"

By the time we arrived at the site, we were well-rehearsed and ready to go. We met the HR and IT managers who gave us a quick tour and led us to the conference room. Within one minute of sitting down, Evans went completely off-script, diving into the features and benefits of Learnit (some of which didn't even exist!). From my perspective, the meeting had gone completely off the rails but instead of jumping in and taking over, I sat there, kept quiet, and let Evans do her thing, curious to see where it might lead. Even though I was probably as confused as the potential customers by what Evans was saying. I could tell they liked her, found her energy contagious, and thought she came across as authentic. Evans finished up her whirl-wind presentation and the HR manager finally got a chance to speak. "Evans," she said, "thanks for all the info; we are going to start with a $25,000 investment from our company in your training services."

We stopped at a Mexican restaurant down the street for tacos and to recap the meeting. I laughed, shook my head, and said, "I'm not exactly sure what just transpired in there, but great job!" Evans, I am happy to say, continues to be a top-producing senior sales executive at Learnit, and the accounting firm remains one of our longest-standing and best customers.

Another important distinction is between being a manager and a coach. Managers give directions to employees, which usually amounts to assigning a task and a due date. A coach, by contrast, doesn't want to hand out all the answers. It's better in the long run to encourage your employees to figure them out on their own. Allowing people to think through problems and roadblocks builds experience and bolsters confidence. Insisting that employees come up with their solutions doesn't mean that you abandon them, however. It's a coach's job to work with them through whatever situations may arise.

If a team member comes to me with an issue or challenge, it would be easy for me to just rattle off advice or tell them what exactly to do. But that wouldn't teach them anything. I prefer to ask open-ended questions and get them to talk through the situation. I ask them to tell me a little bit about the situation, about possible solutions, and the reasoning behind them. This may seem time-consuming, especially if it's a problem you've dealt with dozens of times. But if you put in the work leading your people through the decision-making process, you're helping them learn and develop skills that will pay off for you—and for them—in the long run.

Ideally you want to lead your employees to an appropriate answer. (Often you will be surprised that they come up with solutions even better than you imagined!) It should feel as if you reached a conclusion together, or even that they solved the problem themselves. When people come away from a conversation feeling like they've discovered the answer on their own, they're more likely to buy into the process and their self-confidence is boosted. The fact that you worked the problem alongside them just goes to show that your organization is a place where people are heard and work together toward a common goal. Employees want to work for leaders who are willing to roll up their sleeves and put in the work. They don't want managers who are distant and incapable of being supportive. And if you've hired learn-it-alls, they don't want to just have the answers handed to them. They want coaches.

LEARN TO COACH

The learn-it-all leader strives to ensure their employees are continuously learning and practicing their skills. They also make certain that they're continuously learning and improving their own skills to prepare for even greater leadership success in the future. You can't neglect your own development. I try to always be on the lookout for ways to improve as a coach and leader. Books are a great resource (and I'm thrilled you're reading this one), but they're not enough on their own. If you want to be the best coach you can be, you need to gather information from as many sources as possible.

I'm lucky enough to know a lot of great leaders, and I'm not afraid to ask them questions and learn from their insights on what has contributed to their success. Several high-powered business leaders I know are mentors of mine. They're people I can ask for advice or to challenge me on decisions I'm considering.

SEEK MENTORS. BE A COACH.

As you grow more confident in your leadership abilities and you rack up experience and wins, people may come to you for advice and mentorship. I've mentored several individuals over the years and consider it an honor that they turn to me for mentorship. I've also found coaching other leaders hones my own leadership skills.

I had the great fortune of playing for some legendary baseball coaches, and I've already talked about many of the great lessons I learned from them that I later applied to my role as a business leader. But the truth is, I also had some coaches who weren't so great, and I learned from them as well. Counterexamples are powerful (if unpleasant) teaching tools. Just as you can learn what to do by watching a great coach, you can also see what *not* to do by studying the faults of a bad one. I've had coaches who made my experience miserable but left me with two great "don't do" takeaways: don't take credit for wins that aren't yours and don't be an a**shole.

A particular coach I had liked to put himself at the center of attention when we were playing well. It was all his great coaching decisions that led us to victory. (It was really the efforts of his talented team.) The same coach would turn on a dime during losing streaks and place all the blame on his players to the media with comments like, "How are we expected to win when our cleanup hitter (that was me) has one hit in his last fifteen at-bats?" Great leaders do the opposite; they support and defend their team during losing streaks and shoulder the blame themselves.

The second Don't Do I picked up was from a coach who was extremely negative. Bad coaches focus exclusively on their players' weaknesses and, even worse, call them out in front of their peers. I have never found shaming a team member into working harder or doing better work to be a productive leadership approach. I'm not saying you need to be overly positive at all times—it's important to address weaknesses—but doing so in a positive manner dramatically improves the chances your team members will respond the way you want them to.

If you want people to buy into the idea of being a member of a team working toward a single goal, then you need to do whatever you can to ensure that they feel like they belong. You have to encourage them when they're down and ensure that any criticism you give them is constructive and isn't taken personally. Since you've likely recruited some people with a low level of experience but a high level of untapped talent, it's your job to support them and build their confidence.

LEARN TO INSPIRE

You don't have to be a great motivational speaker or someone with an over-the-top personality to be a great leader, but you do need to be able to inspire your team. A lot of people focus too much on style when they want to be inspiring, but effective leaders have a wide range of personalities. Yes, many leaders are extroverted and charismatic, but there are plenty who are soft-spoken and are just as (or even more) effective. For introverts interested in leadership,

Susan Cain's book *Quiet: The Power of Introverts in a World That Can't Stop Talking* is an absolute must-read. It would be a bad idea for you to try and be the stereotypical gregarious leader if that's not your true personality. If you take a genuine interest in your employees' well-being and focus on your own strengths, you can be a great leader with a style that's authentic to your personality.

The real key to inspirational leadership isn't style. What really inspires people is a leader with a big, compelling vision for the future who lives in accordance with their values and walks their talk by modeling what they want to see. People want to work for leaders who believe in what they're doing, lead by example, and are laser-focused on the vision and purpose they set for themselves and their teams. The loftier your goals and the more sincere your belief that great things are possible, the more inspired your team will become. I was always inspired by my father's vision and how hard he worked to make it happen. That kind of "make it happen" attitude is what great coaches seek to instill in the people that they lead. But perhaps the most effective (and certainly the most inevitable, for good or ill) way to lead is by example.

PEOPLE BELIEVE WHAT YOU DO, NOT WHAT YOU SAY.

If you want your team members to be passionate, show them your passion. If you want hard workers, work hard. You can't inspire a team if you're phoning it in. An inspiring coach-leader needs to be excited about the work they're doing. Project the traits you want to see reflected in your people. It's an exercise in integrity, solidifies your position as a leader, and teaches your team members what you expect from them in the most powerful way possible.

LEARN FROM COACHING

Of course, the primary goal of any coach is to improve the team. But taking on the role of coach has plenty of benefits for you as a learn-it-all leader. Teaching others forces you to look at ideas in new ways. Richard Feynman codified this idea in his eponymous learning technique widely summarized as "if you want to master something, teach it."[23]

Real learning isn't about memorizing facts (we have Google for that); it's about finding ways to make those facts relevant to yourself and others. Coaching, teaching, and sharing what you learn force you to be more thoughtful. Simply knowing that you will later need to coach others on it changes how you approach new material. When you coach somebody, pay attention to how they're receiving the information. Stop and think about the best way to present what you're teaching. Doing so refines your own understanding and helps theirs move along more quickly.

Too often people read books or attend workshops without having a game plan. As a leader, one way to increase your own retention of books or workshops is to go into them with a plan for how you'll take what you learn, apply it to a specific situation, and (when possible) "teach it back" to the people who are in it with you. Having your team members read and discuss a book with you is a great way to expose them to new information while deepening your own experience of the material. Taking information that you've learned and passing it on to others is a skill that can take some time to sharpen, but it's well worth the effort and pays off for you, your employees, and your organization.

---

23 Feynman was a brilliant theoretical physicist nicknamed "the great explainer" for his ability to make the most complex ideas accessible to laypeople with wit and respect. His technique was extrapolated from his notebooks and is summarized nicely here: https://fs.blog/feynman-learning-technique/.

As a leader and a coach, the impact that you have on people's lives is enormous. Leaders who don't acknowledge this and feel no responsibility for the welfare of their team will end up on the losing end of things in the long run. It's something that I've always taken extremely seriously, and it drives me to continue learning, developing, and growing. The employees at Learnit put a lot of trust in me, and I have a responsibility to see that they develop and grow in their jobs. I don't take credit for their success but I am proud of and gratified by how much the team has been rewarded for the hard work, dedication, and continuous learning I've had a hand in coaching.

CHAPTER SUMMARY

Learn-it-all leaders are always learning about leadership from their own experiences, from other leaders, and from the people they lead. They recognize leadership is a process rather than a destination, one which keeps them engaged, humble, and curious. These personal attributes give them the courage and ability to take action, make bold decisions, build great teams and cultures, play to win, and constantly learn to be a coachable coach and a lifetime student.

CONCLUSION

At our annual company retreat in early 2020, there was quite a lot of buzz about our upcoming twenty-fifth anniversary. Learnit would hit the quarter-century mark on June 5, and everyone was wondering how we were going to outdo the legendary party we'd thrown for our twentieth anniversary.[24]

But as the year rolled on, between the pandemic's spread across the world and the civil unrest, nobody felt much like celebrating. Since it was also becoming increasingly obvious that we weren't going to be able to come together in person anyway, we made plans for a day-long virtual get-together. It would be a low-key, no-outsiders event. We scheduled a workshop on diversity and inclusion for the morning followed by a virtual lunch with the afternoon set aside for virtual games, concluding with a virtual happy hour.

The afternoon before the "party" I was feeling uninspired by the plan and started wondering if there was more we could do for the

---

24   We take our celebrations seriously at Learnit! From holiday parties to anniversaries—I'll take any excuse to show our people a good time!

team. I knew a wild party wouldn't be appropriate (or possible) but somehow, what we'd planned didn't feel right either. It lacked energy and enthusiasm. It felt like we weren't going all in.

The more I thought about it, the more I felt like the team needed something a little deeper and more heartfelt. Since the pandemic had started, we'd brought in new people who hadn't yet had the opportunity to really experience the Learnit culture firsthand, and the company deserved more recognition of its history at such a significant milestone than it'd get with our current plan. I didn't say anything to anyone, but I spent the rest of the afternoon sending out emails and making calls, texting some people, and reaching out to others on LinkedIn.

At three-thirty, near the end of the virtual games, faces that not everyone knew started popping up in the Zoom window. By three-forty-five, my frenzy of calls had paid off. We had seventy Learnit alumni and staff on the call. The "room" was full of entrepreneurs, individuals in senior leadership roles at companies of all sizes, a variety of professional artists, a business school dean, and even a few married couples who'd first met at Learnit.

We spent the next three hours telling Learnit stories that spanned its entire twenty-five years. There were funny stories of heroic triumphs and ridiculous ones of newbie mistakes. There were heartfelt accounts of teamwork and moving ones about what the company has meant to people in their professional and personal lives.

I left at six-thirty with people still on the call, drinks in hand, telling stories. I felt incredibly proud to have spent the entire day (and the last twenty-five years) surrounded by such an amazing group of individuals. It was deeply gratifying to see how Learnit had played even a small role in the lives and learning of so many extraordinary people. I couldn't sleep that night for thinking about how proud I was and how proud my dad would have been—of me, of his company, and of what we'd made of his big moon shot dream.

I'd like to say I'd always known it's what Learnit would become, but I didn't. I learned what it could be as it grew and as I learned how to lead it. I learned to be a learn-it-all leader by leading Learnit, and I'm profoundly grateful for the opportunity. I'm also confident that anyone who wants to can learn to be a great leader. That's the reason I wrote this book.

Being a learn-it-all doesn't require you to work at Learnit (although we're always looking for good people!). Being a learn-it-all leader means that any company (or sports team) you lead becomes a company of learners. It starts with your mindset. Great leaders are great students. No matter what your academic background is, you can start where you are. Learn from experience wherever it happens and from everyone you meet.

If you're young and anxious about your abilities, plagued by imposter syndrome, or convinced everyone else has it all figured out, please recognize the enormous advantage you have—you're *not* a know-it-all! If you already have years of experience and confidence in your abilities, and you still finished this book, congratulations! You've protected your learn-it-all mindset from the syndromes most likely to destroy it.

Imposter syndrome and know-it-all-ness (in other words, fear and arrogance) are the opposite but twin enemies of learning. Happily, they're both defeated by the same things—by going all in, staying humble, getting curious, and being principled. When you go all in on learning, you commit to bigger dreams and set a bolder vision. You break that vision into inspiring goals that set the direction for yourself and your teams and keep you focused, moment-by-moment, on the present and the learning it offers.

When you're fully committed to learning, you become willing to take advice and fiercely defend your beginner's mind even as your confidence grows. You engage with the world from a place of curiosity, open yourself to a diversity of perspectives, and ask the questions that both surface opportunities and keep your thinking (but not your ethics) flexible.

Learn-it-all leaders safeguard their values and do the right thing both in their interactions with others and in the way they manage themselves. They give people their respect, attention, forgiveness, and trust, and earn their own respect by behaving with integrity and in accordance with their values. They do this because it's the right thing to do and because they know that we see the world as we are and learn best when we believe the best of ourselves and others.

Being engaged, humble, curious, and principled positions learn-it-all leaders to lead from a position of flexibility *and* strength, able to make bold "screw it, let's do it" decisions *and* carefully considered ones. They don't fall victim to paralysis by analysis because they're certain of a positive outcome—learning—even when things don't go as planned.

Learn-it-all leaders assemble diverse teams of coachable players who share the learn-it-all traits and their company's values and create a culture for them that fosters and supports ongoing learning. They play for big wins as a team without sacrificing their humanity and with an eye to win-win victories, and they coach their players with the same integrity—leading by example and through inspiration so that everyone continues learning and the spiral of success it drives.

When Bert Strane and I reached out to ballplayers to join the charity event we hosted in honor of my father, we contacted people we'd played with and against. Likewise, when we celebrated Learnit's twenty-fifth anniversary, we were joined by present and past teammates. In both instances, the special occasion expanded the definition of "team."

I may not know you, but you've now shared in my wins and losses, my experience, and my education. In these pages, we've been learn-it-alls together, and I'm proud to be on your team. Reach out. Tweet the coolest thing you learned here (or anywhere!) using the hashtag #LearnItAll, and I'll respond. If you see me at a conference or a ballgame, please say hello. I'm curious about my readers and always happy to meet another learn-it-all.

I sincerely hope you enjoy your life as a learn-it-all, living as Gandhi recommended as if you were to die tomorrow but learning as if you were to live forever.[25]

---

25   In *The Good Boatman*, his biography, Rajmohan Gandhi explains his famous father believed "that a man should live thinking he might die tomorrow but learn as if he would live forever." Rajmohan Gandhi, *The Good Boatman: A Portrait of Gandhi* (New Delhi, India: Viking, 1995), 311.

ACKNOWLEDGMENTS

First and foremost, I want to start by thanking my wife Cara for her love, persistence, and confidence in pushing me to write this book. This project was much harder than I originally anticipated, and Cara was always there to hear me out and encourage me to continue and do the very best I could. With her support, I put forth my best effort.

A huge thank you to my mom and dad for being the best parents any kid could have asked for and to my siblings: Sammy, Chelsea, and Taylor. I feel blessed to have you as my family. You have sat through countless hours of listening patiently about Learnit and have been unfailingly supportive. It's an incredible feeling to know you have a family who "has your back" and would do anything to help. Thank you; I couldn't have written this book without you. Especially you, Sammo, for keeping the secret and always being there to review and give constructive feedback on every page and story of the manuscript. Before I move on, I can't forget the most loyal family member of all, my buddy Pablo (my fifteen-year-old puggle). We've been through a lot together.

Special thanks to my friends and colleagues: Kandis Porter and Nick Silverthorn who were both there with me from the beginning of this project, reading every page and not being afraid to tell me when something was lame or needed to be improved. Your feedback was instrumental in helping me through this project.

Matt Murawski, Evans Hood, and Courtney Ritchie: thank you for essentially dedicating the bulk of your professional career to Learnit. I'm so fortunate to have the three of you not only as teammates but also as close friends. We have all grown up together in the past fifteen-plus years, professionally and personally. What a journey! Matt—thanks for being so wonderful to my sister (Chelsea) and your kids. From an older brother's standpoint, I couldn't have gotten luckier than I did with you.

To my brothers-in-law, Garrett and Grant Quibell, thank you for your incredible support. Garrett, for the time you spent at Learnit and for all your innovative ideas, and Grant, for letting me test out my sales theories on you. It's been great to be part of your family. Thanks for welcoming me with open arms. I am three-for-three in the brother-in-law department, that is a fact!

Thanks to my (extended) Learnit crew: Jose Castro, Laurel Taylor, Sarah Finchum, Mary Bussi, Jennifer Albrecht, Toby DeChant, Britt Miller, Dalit Lewis, Jim Mollé, Cara Clifford, Jamie and Garrett Tadlock, Erin Finnegan, Sebastian Goodwin, Brandon Abbey, Summer Taddonio, Nicole Pelky, Joe Fitzpatrick, Jim Hallihan, Will Whittle, Alex Mozes, Todd Lammle, Sherwood Cornforth, Gary Clarke, Josh Mitchell, Bill Taylor, Kevin Landry, Harlan Kilmon, John Robie, and Cathy Epstein. Thank you to Darren Tappen, Joe Angeleta, Lisa and Rob Eyerkuss, Sean Bugler, Mouwafac Sidaoui, Alonzo Jennings, Andy Robbins, Jason Fu, Lamonte Brown, Stewart McDougall,

Matt Aberbacht, Colin Kehn, Almir Guimaraes, Wendy Means, and so many others. What an incredible journey! I'm just taking this moment to think about all the friendships and great stories (some of which are truly hard to believe) I have with each and every one of you. It's pretty amazing if you think about it.

Vince Bigone, Bert Strane, Don Russo, and Bill Sexton, thank you for keeping my father's memory alive through your own childhood stories and being there for me and my family all these years.

To David Chesnosky, Fred Wolfgramm, Dan Toothman, Scott Evars, and Carl Hanson—from Little League baseball to the present day, thanks for an amazing forty-plus-year friendship. And to all our dads—may we emulate them on and off the field with our own children.

Jacob Cruz—thanks for befriending me that first week of fall practice at ASU. Having a team leader and All-American like you as a friend made me feel like I belonged on the team. I will never forget our season-long battle for the batting title that you eventually won! You have been a great friend all these years and are like a brother to me.

Zach Siegel—you were there with Big W even before Learnit opened its doors, and I am grateful to you for taking me under your wing when I arrived on the San Francisco workforce scene.

Steve Mizel, thank you for introducing me to the Canyon Ranch family back in 2008. It's become like a second family to me and such an integral part of my life.

I based several of my stories and learnings on the really unique opportunity I had to play for Andy Lopez, John Noce, and Jim Brock.

I'm forever grateful for what those legendary gentlemen taught me on and off the field. I need to also thank my high school baseball coach, John DeVos, who passed away in late 2022. Coach DeVos was the first to believe in my ability in high school and I am forever grateful for him.

Skyler Gray—my book coach on this journey who spent endless hours working with me on this project. Thank you for never getting frustrated with me. You have the patience of a saint and it was really fun working together.

To Darren Bridgett, the most courageous person I have met. Thank you for showing me the past two years how to deal with adversity and never lose faith. You are an inspiration.

And finally, to my current team at Learnit—I have been at this for twenty-eight-plus years and I have never been more fired up for Learnit than I am at this moment. We have assembled a world-class team of learn-it-alls and I can't wait for what the future will bring!